Tales from Herefordshire's Graves and Burials

Tales from Herefordshire's Graves and Burials

by

Nicola Goodwin

Logaston Press

LOGASTON PRESS
Little Logaston Woonton Almeley
Herefordshire HR3 6QH
Logastonpress.co.uk

First published by Logaston Press 2005
Copyright © Nicola Goodwin 2005

ISBN 1 904396 44 5

Set in New Baskerville, Oxford and Times by Logaston Press
and printed in Great Britain by
Bell & Bain Ltd., Glasgow

Contents

Introduction & Acknowledgements

I've been fascinated by churches and graveyards since I was a pupil at St Mary's School in Fownhope. We spent a lot of time looking at the history and design of the church, but I was always far more interested in reading the gravestones and memorials. For a number of years I used to occasionally pop into a church or graveyard and just read about some of the people who had lived in the area. As I discovered more and more intriguing stories and mysteries the idea for compiling and sharing them in this book seemed a natural progression. Researching the book was very enjoyable and deepened my knowledge and love of my home county of Herefordshire. Rather than solving questions and mysteries though I seem to have uncovered many more puzzles from the past; enough to keep me enjoying the delights of the county's churches for many years to come!

Having said that, there are a number of burials included within this book for which I have found scant information and are therefore something of a mystery, for example that of Edmund John Jones at Breinton, those of the small children who died in the summer of 1870 at Little Hereford, or why several members of the Bird family of Mordiford died on the same day in 1818, or who do the picture stones at Norton Canon commemorate and, in the same churchyard, who was the friend of Sarah Parry and why was she so worried as to what might happen to her remains. For others there appears to be quite a lot of information, some of which can no longer be checked, but which appears to give conflicting evidence for whose tomb we may be looking at, for example the 'Clifford' tomb in Aconbury church. Others are simply mysterious—like what did happen to Mrs. Oliver of Holmer? And then, whose tomb is that at Munsley that might be marked with the name Hamlet? If anyone has information which might help solve any of these mysteries, then please contact me c/o Logaston Press, or via my BBC address: nicola.goodwin@bbc.co.uk.

This book would not have been written if it hadn't been for the help of a number of people. Thank you to the numerous members of the church, parishioners and churchwardens who have helped and accompanied me during my visits. Without the assistance of the staff at Hereford Library and the county archives office much of my research would not have been possible, and thank you also to the many listeners of BBC Hereford and Worcester who contacted me with suggestions for the book. Andy Johnson of Logaston Press has been incredibly patient and good-humoured during the lengthy process of editing and publishing and deserves a big drink! Sadly one of my biggest contributors did not live long enough to see this book published, but thank you to my dear friend Albert Daniels who, during his 98 years as a Herefordian, met many of the characters featured in these pages. His amazing memory and good humour helped me bring many of the former residents of the county to life.

Nicola Goodwin
September 2005

ABBEYDORE

The parish church of St Mary at Abbeydore rests on
the site of one of England's most important monasteries.

The enormous building contains two 13th-century effigies of
knights, believed to be those of Robert de Eywas and Roger de
Clifford. The southern ambulatory contains the larger effigy which is
quite badly damaged with its head, shoulders and lower legs missing. It
shows a knight in chain mail with a narrow girdle, a shield over his chest
and drawing a sword from his scabbard with his right hand. This is
thought to be the effigy of Roger de Clifford, but identifying which
Roger de Clifford lies there takes a bit of time as there were three
members of the family who bore the same name and who are all linked
to Abbeydore. To add to the mystery and confusion, the families of
Eywas and Clifford are closely linked through the 13th century.

Roger de Clifford the elder was known as Roger of Tenbury and is
thought to have been born in 1189 and died in 1231 or 1232. His family
seat, Clifford Castle in north-west Herefordshire, played a major part in
the wars between England and Wales in the 12th and 13th centuries with
Roger's ancestors fighting both for and against the crown at different
stages. In 1214 Roger married Sibil de Eywas, the daughter of the second
Robert, Lord of Eywas, and their son, also called Roger, was born in
1231. Roger senior therefore became Lord of Eywas for his lifetime,
uniting both families and becoming a powerful marcher lord. Sibil died
in 1236 aged in her late 40s or early 50s and is likely to have been buried
in the abbey. The effigy in the southern ambulatory is dated too late to
be that of Roger de Clifford senior.

The second Roger was born in 1231 just one year before his father's
death. With his half-brother Robert inheriting the Eywas fortune, he was
left in debt and spent many years working to regain the status of a major

Effigy believed to be that of Roger de Clifford

figure in the political arena and the constant battles between the crown and the country's barons. Roger became Baron Clifford in 1263 after the death of his uncle, part of his inheritance being Eardisley Castle where he imprisoned the bishop of Hereford, Peter de Aquablanca who had fallen out of favour with King Henry III. Roger's support for the king included fighting at the battle of Evesham against de Montfort and he was rewarded with land, the cancellation of debt and the marriage of his son, the third Roger de Clifford, with Isabel, the co-heiress of the barony of Appleby. Roger, the father, was married to the Countess of Loretto, a member of a French noble family who was buried in Worcester Cathedral in 1301.

In *A Definitive History of Dore Abbey*, Ron Shoesmith and Ruth Richardson describe how Roger was fond of cattle-raiding and ill-treating his tenants and later in his life he 'was forced to walk barefoot to the high altar of Hereford Cathedral by Bishop Thomas de Cantilupe with the bishop beating him with a rod'. This second Roger died in either 1284 or 1285 in France and left his body to be buried in the church at Abbeydore. The third Roger pre-deceased his father and died in 1282 and so the effigy in the southern ambulatory could either be him, with the father overseeing the work on his son's tomb, or the second Roger himself. The will of the second Roger proves that he asked to be buried at Dore next to his son, so both men were definitely laid to rest in the abbey even if only one is recognised with an effigy.

The smaller effigy is situated in the northern ambulatory and shows a very similar figure with a knight lying on a raised slab with his head on a cushion, wearing a complete suit of

Tomb built for Peter de Aquablanca at Hereford Cathedral

armour and holding a
shield in his left hand and a broad sword in his
right hand. This effigy is thought to date from 1240 to
1270 and is in the west country style. This is believed to represent Robert of Eywas, but five members of the Eywas family were
named Robert. The first was the founder of the abbey and although
documents show he was buried at the site, the effigy dates more than
a century after his death. His son, the second Robert, was killed in 1196
and is also believed to be buried nearby but, again, his death pre-dates
the effigy.

Sibil, wife of the first Roger de Clifford had first married Robert de
Tregoz who had thus become Lord of Eywas. Robert is thought to have
been buried in Normandy and, although the exact date of his death isn't
known, it's thought to have been too early for the effigy. On Sibil's death
in 1236 her son Robert de Tregoz the second became the lord of Eywas.
He married Juliana, the sister of Thomas Cantilupe who later became
bishop of Hereford and then a saint. He died in 1268 and it may well be
that the effigy in the northern ambulatory is his although it could also
be that of his younger son, who was—of course—also called Robert.

In the Presbytery there is a small effigy on the left wall commemo-
rating the heart burial of John de Breton, bishop of Hereford. He
became bishop in 1269 and held office until his death in 1275.
Previously he served as a canon at the cathedral, was a doctor of laws and
a Keeper of the King's Wardrobe. His body is buried in Hereford
Cathedral but his heart was interred at Dore Abbey so he could be close
to his parents who are also buried at Abbeydore. John de Breton had a
difficult and political time in office. He took over as bishop from the
unpopular Peter de Aquablanca and immediately stopped the previous
common practice of lucrative clerical posts going to the bishops' family

Effigy believed to be that of Robert of Ewyas

3

and friends. Peter de Aquablanca's relatives took de Breton to the papal courts in 1275 and the records say there were physical fights as they tried to retain their seats and power.

The side chapel in the south transept, the Hoskyns Chapel, contains a large stone altar tomb to John Hoskyns (or Hoskins) (1566–1638) whose family can be traced throughout the history of Herefordshire. John Hoskyns was a friend of Sir Walter Raleigh and he was actually imprisoned alongside him in the Tower of London for some time. A well known local story also says that he entertained King James 1 at Morehampton with a Morris Dance carried out by ten local villagers whose combined age totalled exactly one thousand years!

John Hoskyns was an author and many of his books can still be viewed in the Cathedral Library. He was also an MP and a Judge, the brother of a canon at Hereford Cathedral and the first owner of the Morehampton Park estate, situated between Credenhill and Sarnesfield in the north-west of the county, which was passed on through many generations of his family.

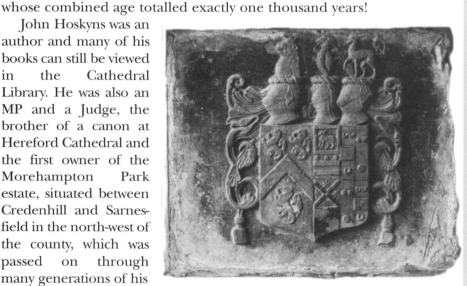

Coat-of-Arms on the Hoskyns' tomb

ACONBURY

The church of St John the Baptist is now unfortunately locked, but the key can be requested through Diocesan officials at Hereford Cathedral and the building is well worth a visit.

The church was originally part of the Sisters of the Order of St John of Jerusalem which was founded in 1237 by Margaret de Lacy. Margaret was given the land at Aconbury by King John after asking for a place where she could build a house in memory of her father, mother and brother. She had failed to realise that the members of the order were liable for service abroad though and, as she didn't approve of this, Margaret wrote to the pope asking that the nuns should be allowed to become members of the Augustinian order. After five years the pope gave his permission and the convent at Aconbury became a community of Augustinian nuns. It was dissolved in 1539.

The 13th-century church is widely believed to be one of England's few haunted churches and local folklore and legend talk of the spirit of a monk who roamed the church and churchyard in his habit and cowl. It's believed that the haunting became so troublesome that a former minister and a number of parishioners captured the spirit in a bottle and buried it within the walls of the church. Local lore says the spirit was thought to have escaped again, but I can assure you that the current tenants of Aconbury Court which sits alongside the church have not yet been troubled by the wandering monk.

The church contains a tomb under the window nearest the door in the small nave which is believed to be that of one of the many Roger de Cliffords (see also the previous entry for Abbeydore). Although the inscription is now difficult to read, parish records show that in 1885 the Reverend F.T. Havergal discovered that the indecipherable inscription was such because the stonemason had laid the paper tracing the wrong side up when carving the tomb. The inscription should have read. 'Here lies Dame Maud de Gorneye. Partner of Sir Roger de Clifford—Pray for Her Soul.' The vault was opened and was found to contain a very large skeleton lying alongside a smaller skull believed to belong to a woman. Dame Maud was the eldest daughter of Roger de Vipont, the Lord of Westmorland. The tomb was closed once again without the remains being disturbed.

Reverend D.E. Jones explores the tomb in his *Aconbury: The Priory, The Church and The Camp.* He believes that the name may actually read 'Sir Walter de Clifford' rather than Roger but, as the inscription has now almost disappeared, it may never be possible to establish whose remains lie at Aconbury. The Clifford family tree may offer one expla-nation as Roger de Clifford, grandson of Roger and Sybil, married Isabel, a co-heiress of the barony of Appleby (again, see the entry for Abbeydore) and their son, also of course called Roger, is referred to as Baron Clifford and Lord of Westmorland. Could the inscription have read: 'Here lies Dame Isabel ...'? It would be logical to assume that he had inherited the Westmorland title from his mother's family. This theory would throw confusion on much of Herefordshire's history, however, because, as you will see in the entry for Abbeydore, the Roger de Clifford who married Isabel died before his father and is believed to be buried in Dore Abbey. Another possibility, for which I can find no factual evidence, is that Reverend Jones is correct and the tomb at

Aconbury is that of a
Walter de Clifford who did indeed marry
Dame Isabel who was in some way related to Isabel,
wife of Roger de Clifford. It would not have been unusual for
siblings to marry into the same family.

The church also contains a memorial to Johanna Pauncefoot on
the floor of the Chancel and many gravestones in the overgrown
churchyard.

ALLENSMORE

St Andrews Church, Allensmore, is well known in the history of the
county for its place in the 'Herefordshire Commotion' of May 1605. At
the time the area was home to a large, very poor squatter community but
they showed their morals and local passion when Alice Wellington, a
catholic, was apparently refused burial at St Andrews, the vicar, Richard
Heyns, giving as the reason that she had died excommunicate from the
Church of England. The villagers were not impressed, and early one
morning more than 50 people processed to the church where they took
it upon themselves to bury Alice.

Three men were eventually arrested over the incident, but two
escaped whilst still in Allensmore and the High Sheriff was forced to free
the third man on his way back to Hereford when he met 50 armed local
men. There were a number of raids and arrests for a further six weeks
before the unrest died down. Alice's grave can no longer be seen but
thanks to her fellow villagers she remains at rest at St Andrews.

Inside the church there is an unusual marble floor-slab which can be
seen in the chancel. This is dedicated to Sir Andrew and Lady Juliana
Herley (in some records shown as Harl) and the inscription and
engraving is well preserved. The slab was recently researched by the
Brass of the month website team who believe it to be one of a small group
of slabs produced in Herefordshire in the 14th and 15th centuries.
Other examples from tis time can be seen in the churches of Canon
Pyon, Dilwyn and in Hereford Cathedral.

Sir Andrew, who died in 1392, is shown in armour with a tight fitting
jupon and he has a lion at his feet. His wife, Juliana, is wearing a low
necked gown edged with fur and in the folds at the bottom of her gown
a small dog wearing a collar and bell can be seen hiding. The slab also
contains ten small coats of arms which include those of the Herley and
Pauncefoot families. The current churchwardens believe the slab may
previously have been on an altar tomb in the north chapel which may
have been the Herley family chapel.

The detail of the dog at Lady Juliana's feet is worth a particular mention and the inlay of the slab is believed to be made of cement, which was highly unusual at the time.

Above the floor slab is a memorial to Mary Ann Duncomb, daughter of John Duncomb, a clerk, and his wife Ann. Mary died on 18 December 1798 aged just six and she's remembered with this poignant poem:

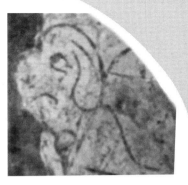

Detail of the dog at Lady Juliana's feet

When the fresh rose-bud, moist with morning dew
All fair appears just bursting into view
Pleas'd hope anticipates its fragrant breath
Nor sees the canker hid within its leaf:
Such the fond hopes this lovely blossom gave
Vain hopes here buried in an early grave!
If youth shall read and beauty gently sigh
Whilst pity's soft effusion fills the eye
O many the thoughts, to useful purpose led.
Teach them with care the path of life to tread
Unknown how long to tread that path is given
Prepar'd to leave it, fix the eye on Heav'n.

At the entrance to the church take a look at the plaque opposite the porch door. This is a memorial to Captain Elliot Blair Crassett who was a member of the 28th Punjabis, a regiment of the Indian Army, who was killed at the battle of Loos on 25 September 1915. He was the son of J.E. Crassett, former vicar of St Andrews.

ASTON INGHAM

The church of St John the Baptist at Aston Ingham, a small parish between Ross-on-Wye and the Gloucestershire border, contains two carved stone coffin lids displayed on either side of the altar. The one lid clearly shows a head with coiffed hair and has a clear floral/trefoil design lower down. The second is not as clear but shows a figure with their hands clasped in prayer. The lids

One of the coffin lids at Aston Ingham

have been identified as
belonging to Sir Thomas de Eston and his wife,
although more recent experts believe the figures
shown may be priests. They are dated from approximately
1300.

Thanks to the research of parishioners, it is known that when Thomas succeeded Simon de Eston, he decided to take the name 'de Eston' after receiving the lordship and church patronage from the Inghayn family. Sir Thomas was granted a knighthood and created Sheriff of Herefordshire, an office that he handed on to his son, Roger. Records show that the estate was run by Roger until he bequeathed it to his son, another Thomas, in approximately 1354. The Lordship was then taken back by the crown for 30 years before being handed to William de Eston (Sir Thomas's great grandson). He was the last of the family to hold the lordship, as Bishop Polton of Hereford ordered the Dean of Ross to hold an enquiry into the right of patronage at Aston Ingham and the property subsequently passed into the hands of the Grendon family.

The chancel also contains brasses to members of the Whatley family.

AVENBURY

The ruined church of St Mary's at Avenbury near Bromyard is one of the county's most historic and religious and is first listed as belonging to a wealthy priest called Sprites in 1066. Sadly the last church there was closed in 1931 and is now just ruins, but does still attract many visitors. The most commonly told story relates to the ghostly organ music which has been heard by many people passing by or using the church as shelter. The Reverend Archer-Shepherd, a former parish priest, recorded hearing the music playing in the empty church and writes of a village story that the mysterious musician was a keen amateur organist who had been killed by his brother at the nearby bridge on the road to Bromyard.

In medieval times Avenbury was also linked to the ghost of Nicholas Vaughan who was reputed to have burned one of the houses belonging to the Bishop of Hereford. He was executed for the crime but is alleged to have returned and haunted the village until his ghost was captured by twelve priests and buried in a silver box under a large stone in the nearby River Frome. I was also told a village tale by a carpenter working for a very elderly brother and sister who have lived in Avenbury since the beginning of the 20th century. They believed that the stone in the river

8

covered the grave of a
wicked woman, probably a witch, whom the
villagers refused to let be buried within the churchyard
and so was laid to rest in the river within sight of the church.
Whatever the truth behind the tale, on summer days a very large
stone can be seen in the river just before the small bridge linking
the footpaths!

Many of the gravestones are still visible amongst the ruins of St Mary's including that of Anne May, the daughter of H. and E.M. Cooke, who died on 30 January 1900 aged 20 months, and Mary Hyde of the Goodships in Avenbury who died on 30 April 1899 aged 72. There are two unusual coffin-shaped stones in memory of members of the Edward family (1852 and 1866) and also the base of crosses to Hannah Elizabeth (Bessie) Baskerville and James Baskerville who died on 11 September 1921 aged 69. They were both members of the Baskerville family from Kington and the Welsh borders who are alleged to have influenced the writing of Sir Arthur Conan Doyle; if only he could have visited the marvellously atmospheric ruins of St Mary's, Avenbury!

AYLTON

The tiny parish church of Aylton (which is not dedicated) contains the tomb of Emma Foulger, a young lady of the parish who met an unfortunate end in 1855. Emma was the daughter of Thomas and Eliza Foulger of Aylton Court, the hamlet's main house which is situated half a mile from the church. On 10 July 1855 Emma, then aged 14, was accidentally shot on the stairs of the hall. She had been running down to greet her brother who had just arrived back from shooting when he is believed to have stumbled and fallen, discharging his shotgun as he did so. According to local rumour, her ghost is still believed to haunt the stairs of Aylton Court.

Emma was buried a few days later but the tragedy continues as her grave was disturbed and her corpse was taken by body snatchers. Despite the introduction of the Anatomy Act in 1832 which legalised the supply of corpses for dissection and medical research, the work of body snatchers or, resurrectionists as they were known, still continued.

Emma's grave is situated at the back of Aylton Church; go up the steps and round to the graveyard and it can be easily found next to the church wall. The damage done by the body snatchers to the stone tablet can be clearly seen but plans are underway to restore the grave.

AYMESTREY

The Church of St John the Baptist and St Alkmund dates from the 14th century and contains memorials to many historic Herefordshire families such as Weever, Lingen and Dunne, but the most historically important grave in the village is believed to lie approximately 200 metres from the churchyard. Here a mass grave was dug for more than 4,000 soldiers killed at the battle of Mortimer's Cross in 1461. A mound can still be seen from the main road as you travel towards the turning for Lucton. The battle, when Edward Mortimer defeated the Lancastrians led by the Earl of Pembroke and prevented them from reaching Ludlow and Wigmore castles, though involving relatively small numbers of troops, proved to be one of the most decisive in the Wars of the Roses. The 19-year-old victor went on to become Edward IV.

BACTON

The monument to Blanche Parry at Bacton

St Faith's Church, Bacton, has long been drawing tourists to this tiny hamlet in the Golden Valley as it contains a remarkable monument to one Blanche Parry. Born in 1508 at New Court in the parish of Bacton, Blanche was part of an important family in the county and through her cousins she became a familiar guest at the royal courts. When Queen Elizabeth was just 3 years old Blanche was made one of her four ladies-in-waiting and she remained unmarried, serving the queen throughout her life. She would have enjoyed a good quality of life for the period, with a rich income plus board and lodging for herself and her own servants at court. She is believed to have become

blind in her last few
years and died in 1589 at the age of 82 with the
queen at her side. Her loyalty was rewarded as the
queen commanded her to be buried with the rank of
Baroness and paid for her funeral and the magnificent monument you can see on the wall of the chantry. Although Blanche's body is interred at St Margaret's Church in Westminster, her internal organs are believed to be contained in the Bacton memorial.

As you enter the church, stop before the door and read the stone tablet just inside the entrance porch. This gives details of Blanche Parry's bequest to her home parish, including yearly amounts of rye and wheat to be distributed to the poor plus money for the upkeep of the church and 20 cattle for the parish. Directly opposite the door inside the church you can see a framed embroidered tapestry by Blanche Parry which was formerly used as an altar cloth in the church.

There are other interesting memorials in St Faith's Church. Behind the altar is a memorial to Daisy Elizabeth Hamp Partridge who died at the age of 21 in 1906 and also to her brother, Reginald Gardener Partridge, who was killed in action in South Africa in 1900 aged just 20. To the right of the door as you leave the church you can see a detailed memorial to Alexander Stanter (1620) and Rachel Stanter (1663) which shows them kneeling towards each other with him resplendent in doublet and hose and his wife holding a skull. Mrs Stanter was born Rachel Hopton, the daughter of Sir Arthur Hopton. Interestingly, county records show that Bacton was such a poor parish in the early 17th century that the parishioners could not afford a

priest. Instead, more than 500 peasants worshipped in a chapel provided by Rowland Vaughan of Newcourt Farm (previously the home of Blanche Parry). It's possible, therefore, that the commissioning of the Stanter monument may have been delayed until the parish priest returned and the church was once again in regular use.

The Stanter memorial

BARTESTREE

St Michael's Convent at Bartestree has recently been converted into unusual flats and apartments but the developers have left some poignant reminders of the building's former life. The garden of remembrance contains dozens of graves to the former nuns who spent their lives at Bartestree, whilst the founder of the neighbouring hospice, Freda Pearce, is buried with her husband on the left hand side of the graveyard. Freda Pearce began the hospice in 1984 to offer care to terminally ill people of Herefordshire, having previously been a stalwart of the county's charitable work, raising thousands of pounds for cancer charities in particular.

The small walled garden in the bottom corner of the grounds is difficult to access but was previously the last resting place for the 'fallen women' who lived at the convent. The foreman in charge of the convent re-development cleared the site when work began but it soon became overgrown again. He believed that there were as many as 40 graves in the small plot, some containing basic wooden crosses but the majority completely unmarked. The future of this small patch of ground is still uncertain.

BISHOP'S FROME

St Mary's at Bishop's Frome contains a very rare painted memorial in the Munderfield Chapel. The painting on wood shows Margery, daughter of John Pychard of Paunton, and her husband George de la Downes. They married in 1560 and Margery died in 1598. She is shown kneeling facing her husband who is wearing armour, and beneath them is a tomb with a skeleton on the lid. The painting has been recently restored and is believed to be one of only a few memorials of this kind in England. The discovery of the painting in 2003 came a surprise to the parishioners but they are determined to preserve it for future generations.

Knight Templar effigy at Bishop's Frome

St Mary's also contains
an effigy of a Knight Templar who is shown with
a dog at his feet, the traditional sign that he returned
home safely from the crusades. The effigy has a damaged foot
but is otherwise intact and is on the right of the nave by the pulpit.
It's believed to date from the 13th century.

BISHOPSTONE

The Church of St Lawrence at Bishopstone is situated just out of the main village and dates mainly from the 13th century. The side chapel contains a tomb chest to John Berington who died on 5 February 1613 and his wife Joyce. They are portrayed by stone effigies on top of the tomb chest, their hands clasped in prayer, and in formal dress carved in great detail. John Berington has a dog at his feet, whilst the tomb chest has a blue coloured surround and is decorated with coats of arms and shields.

The sanctuary has a black marble and alabaster monument to Sarah Freer containing an angel figure which was erected by her children. On the wall of the nave is an unusual stone oval plaque to Frances Parler who died in infancy on 17 January 1753 aged 6 weeks: 'Death from sin, have set her free, As she died in her infancy.' There is also a rather more recent wall tablet to Humphrey Adam Gilbert (1885–1960): 'Barrister. Cricketer. Ornithologist. Fisherman and Author. 'To all the world a universal friend.'

BODENHAM

St Michael and All Angel's in Bodenham is a large village church, the chantry of which contains a very simple stone effigy of a woman, believed to be a member of the Devereux family, and her baby. The late 14th-century tomb is simply carved but contains some very good detail, especially on her nails and hair and the features of the child. There is no inscription but Sir Walter Devereux was Lord of Bodenham Manor in the latter 14th century and village records indicate that the tomb is that of his wife.

Effigy of a woman and her baby at Bodenham

13

The church also contains a mural tablet to the Reverend John Pember who led a tumultuous life. He was vicar of Bodenham for 50 years from his installation in 1627, with the exception of a brief period from 1646 when he was ejected by Cromwell. He became a Prebendary of Hereford Cathedral. The unusual memorial is a bronze inscription with a stone surround, and is to the right of the altar. The memorial was installed by his son, also Reverend John Pember, who was the Prebendary at St David's Cathedral in Wales.

BOSBURY

Holy Trinity Church, Bosbury, contains the grave of one of Herefordshire's historical novelists. Emily Lyall, who wrote under the pen name of Ada Edna Bayley, is the author of *In Spite Of All* a historical novel about the Civil War based in the county which was published in 1901. Described as one of the country's most 'progressive novelists,' she died in 1903. Her brother was vicar of Bosbury at the time of her death. Her gravestone markings can now barely be seen, but her grave is marked by a small stone cross next to the old preaching cross adjacent to the church path.

BREDWARDINE

The ancient church of St Andrew's, Bredwardine, is thought to date from the time of the Norman conquest and is nestled on the banks of the River Wye. The small and tranquil church grounds back on to traditional orchards and contain the last resting place of one of Herefordshire's most famous residents, the Reverend Francis Robert Kilvert.

As you enter the churchyard, you'll pass a modern stone seat dedicated to Kilvert under the large yew tree. Turn left and walk around the northern side of the church. Kilvert's grave is marked by a white marble cross and the cleric is surrounded by the villagers described so vividly in his diaries. The simple marble memorial to Kilvert who died aged 38 on 23 September 1879 contains two quotations: 'Until the day break, and the shadows flee away' from Canticles 11.17 and 'He being dead yet speaketh' from the Epistle to the Hebrews.

Francis Kilvert was a simple cleric whose life was sadly cut short by illness just one month after his marriage to Elizabeth Rowland (she too is buried at Bredwardine, her white marble memorial is in the more modern graveyard, situated to the southern side of the church in the top right hand corner). He ministered at Bredwardine from November 1877 until his death, but the wonderfully vivid descriptions of life in the border county, both here and around Clyro where he was curate for several years, have been enjoyed by thousands of people across the world since the first publication of his diaries in 1938. Kilvert's modest memorial is a fitting tribute to the cleric who thought his writing to be merely a record of a simple and uninteresting life, but whose diaries have brought to life the day by day joy and tragedy of life in the borders during Victorian times.

A poignant passage in Kilvert's diary recalls how he visited the home of David Davies, a shepherd, and his wife, Margaret, at the Old Weston, and prayed for their son, 8-year-old Davie. He recounts how Davie had seemed eerily to predict his own death and foresee the details of his own funeral, and describes how Davie's death reminded him of the earlier death of his own young sister. Davie was buried on Christmas Day 1878, and his newly restored grave is situated about ten metres away from Kilvert's, in the north-west of the churchyard.

Crossing over to the southern side of the churchyard brings another heart-warming tale from the past of rural Bredwardine. If you walk out of the church porch directly south you come to a large tomb topped by a slanted stone. This is the final resting place of George Jarvis, a tramp who returned from making his fortune in America as a leather merchant to remember the good folk of the village who had taken pity on him in earlier times. Jarvis died on 12 February 1793 aged 94 and bequeathed money to the parishes of Bredwardine, Staunton-on-Wye and Letton to provide assistance for the poor and needy. The residents of the three villages were believed to have been the most generous to Jarvis during his tramping days, so they benefited from his donation but Brobury villagers, just across the river, received nothing after withholding their charity.

In the new section of the graveyard to the south of the church (across the path leading to the former Vicarage) there are two more interesting memorials. In the top corner is the grave of Kilvert's wife Elizabeth and along the left wall of this section is a flat, raised grave belonging to Major General Pitman of the 11th Hussars who died in 1941. The ledger stone was once topped by a bronze replica of his dress uniform but this has since been removed. The bronze was sculpted by Madame Sabatini, wife of the author Raphael Sabatini who lived for a time at nearby Clock Mill (she is also mentioned in the entry for Hay on Wye).

BREINTON

St Michael's Church at Breinton contains a wealth of unusual gravestones both within and outside its walls. Inside the church in the bottom corner of the nave next to the unused west door is a wooden memorial to Captain Rudhall Booth. Rudhall, who was a descendant of Bishop Booth of Hereford, died in Barwick-upon-Tweed on 29 October 1685 aged 24. His family were heavily involved in the English Civil War fighting for the crown, and he was Commander-in-Chief of the Holy Island garrison. He died of a violent fever on the island and is buried under the chancel steps in St Michael's. His memorial is a large square painted wooden tablet decorated with the family crest and the initials R.B. The colours and images

are still very clear and the inscription can be easily read: 'He always lived a Godly life (and so well prepared as not to feare to dye)'. Rudhall's brother, Charles, fled into exile in France with James II and later died in France. His son, also called Charles, could not return to Breinton to claim the estate as he had renounced the English government under William and Mary, but the family's land was eventually leased to the dean and vicar's choral of Hereford through secret conveyancing.

As you leave the church, head directly south and you will find a very unusual gravestone marking the last resting place of Canon Charles Vincent Gorton. The large cross contains a short line of musical notes from Elgar's Oratorio *The Apostles* and is one of only two such monuments in the country. Canon Gorton (9 July 1854–20 August 1912) was the co-founder of the Morecambe Music Festival and a Canon at Manchester Cathedral. In 1903 Edward Elgar was asked to write a piece of music for the festival and

The gravestone of Canon Charles Vincent Gordon, with a detail of the bar of music from Elgar's The Apostles *(right)*

the pair became friends,
with the Gortons staying with Elgar during
their visits to the Three Choirs Festival. Canon Gorton
came to live in Herefordshire after retiring, but tragically
drowned in the River Wye just days before the 1912 Three Choirs
Festival in which Elgar returned from his new home in London to
conduct *The Dream of Gerontius*. The only other gravestone which
contains the very same notes belongs to the co-founder of the
Morecambe Festival who is buried in Cumbria.

As you move around the west end of the church there is a large gravestone right alongside the unused west door. This belongs to Charles
Hassard Wilfred Dodgson who lived at Breinton House and died in
1941. His close relative was rather more well known, as he changed his
name from Dodgson to Lewis Carroll and became famous for the *Alice
in Wonderland* books.

Continue round the edge of the church and there is a wealth of
unusual gravestones. Halfway along the outside of the nave wall just
below the window, is the grave of James Cranston, an architect who
played a major part in the restoration of the church in 1866. He was also
a founder member of the West of England Rose Society and his grandfather, John Cranston, founded the large nurseries at Kings Acre in
Hereford. James's father Thomas, and his uncle, also James, planted
nearly all of the cedar trees in Herefordshire and they are buried on the
southern side of the churchyard beneath, aptly, the cedar of Lebanon. It
seems odd that James chose to be buried so far from the rest of his
family, but the nearby window is dedicated to him so maybe he's keeping
a close eye on its safety.

Just behind the Cranston gravestone are many graves of the du
Buisson family. The Reverend Edmund du Buisson, who inspired the
restoration of the church, also has a window in memory of him. One of
the graves has a bishop's crosier carved in stone on the top in memory
of Henry Victor, Edward's grandson and the bishop of Lebombo Land
from 1936 to 1949. He died in September 1962 aged 78.

Over towards the eastern edge of the graveyard, near the former
rectory now known as Breinton Grange, is a puzzling mystery. Here is a
tiny coffin-shaped stone in memory of Edmund John, son of John Edwin
Jones. The stone lies next to the graves of Edmund Lewis (who died on
9 September 1844 aged 67) and Susan Lewis (who died on 26 August
1875 aged 84) and their son John Lewis (who died on 3 January 1842
aged 15). Why is another family's child lying at the foot of their graves
or was there a mistake by the stonemason that was never corrected?

BRILLEY

St Mary's Church at Brilley stands on top of the hill looking down on the English/Welsh border and the River Wye below. Inside the well-maintained church are two unusual cast iron grave-slabs; very similar to the ones at Burrington Church. The slabs use the sans serif style of lettering many years before it became popular and widely used across the country. The slabs originally stood outside the east end of the church and covered the graves of Guilbert Hare of Brilley Court who died on 13 February 1669 and his daughter Margaret Hare who died on 22 March 1669. Guilbert's wife was

The iron tombstone of Guilbert Hare now inside the church

Jane Walker who was the daughter of the Shropshire ironmaster Francis Walker. In 1643 Francis Walker had cast nearly a thousand pounds of artillery which was used by the field army in Shropshire. The iron graves of Jane Hare and their second daughter Maria Hare can be seen alongside her relatives the Walker family at Burrington. Both the iron stones can be seen just inside the church door and are now preserved from the elements.

There is also a more modern iron cross which originally stood on the grave of John Walter Lee, vicar of Brilley and Michaelchurch from 1873 until 1887 when he died aged 58.

BROCKHAMPTON

(near Ross-on-Wye)

The Church of All Saints, Brockhampton, is itself a monument. Built in 1902, it was designed by W.R. Lethaby, a member of the Arts and Crafts movement founded by William Morris. The original church is situated at the back of Brockhampton Court and is now part of the private nursing home, but All Saints was created at the request of Mrs Alice Foster, a former resident of the Court who wanted a church designed in memory of her parents, Ebenezer and Julia Jordan. The foundation stone was laid on 25 June 1901 and the church was consecrated in October 1902.

At the back of the church in the top corner by the tree is a modern gravestone in memory of Ralph Godwin Yarnold who died in 1998 aged 84. Ralph Yarnold is a wonderful example of a modern village tale as he was the 'Colonel's Runner'. Brockhampton Cricket Club, whose ground can be seen from the church, prides itself on being a traditional village club as well as one of the county's most successful sides. Back in the 1920s, young Ralph Yarnold learned the skills of the game by being the extra 'player' in the first team. 'The Colonel', the nickname for the Reverend Arthur Wellesley Foster, the husband of Alice and the master of Brockhapmton Court, was a member of the team. He was obsessed by the game of cricket and was well known for hiring staff according to their cricketing ability rather than for their other skills. He even granted the tenancies of farms to talented players to persuade them to move to Brockhampton. Either the Colonel's own cricketing days were long behind him or he thought it beneath him to be seen exerting himself, so young Ralph would crouch behind him in the field and run after any balls that came his way, before returning the ball to the Colonel who would throw the ball to the wicketkeeper and claim any success from Ralph's fielding. Whether any visiting teams dared to complain about the twelve 'men' on the field is not recorded!

BROMYARD

The large parish church of St Peter's in Bromyard contains the Avenbury Knight, a 13th-century stone coffin lid which was originally placed in St Mary's Church at nearby Avenbury, but was moved to St Peter's when the village church was closed and began to fall into ruin. It is approximately 8 feet long and almost a foot thick in places and contains the remarkably well preserved carving of a knight. He is shown in full armour facing forwards with his leg at a right angle, and is holding a sword and a shield. It is well worth searching out the coffin lid, which is tucked away in the north-west corner of the church behind the children's play area.

BURGHILL

The church of St Mary the Virgin, Burghill, contains two interesting brass memorials from the early 17th century. Both brasses are now positioned within the sanctuary rails on the north wall of the chancel.

The earlier brass is to John Awbrey who died on 11 June 1616 aged 38. He is depicted next to his wife Rachell, kneeling at a prayer desk with their son and daughter behind them. John Awbrey was a Doctor of law and a Master of Requests to Queen Elizabeth. His father, William Awbrey, a former Chancellor to Archbishop Whitgift, lived at Burlton Court near the village.

The globe on Robert Masters's brass memorial at Burghill

The second brass contains a small rectangular plate featuring a small terrestrial globe on a stand and is a memorial to Robert Masters, one of the early great voyagers. Masters, who died on 3 June 1619, had sailed with Sir Richard Grenville's expedition of 1585 to form a colony in Virginia. In 1586 Masters and Thomas Cavendish set out on their own expedition to explore the South Seas and in the process they succeeded in circumnavigating the globe; some nine years after Drake's epic voyage. It's believed that Robert purchased the Manor of Burghill on his return in 1596 and the family lived there until 1702. Many of Robert Masters' descendants are buried in the chancel near the brass.

The links between the Cavendish voyages and Herefordshire are numerous. One account of the 1596 journey was written by Robert Hues, a mathematician born in Little Hereford, who accompanied Cavendish and Masters.

Masters was also a friend of Francis Godwin, Bishop of Hereford from 1617 to 1633, who wrote *The Man In The Moone*, a story of a 17th-century voyage to the moon and the people the voyagers encountered there. Bishop Godwin's story was an instant success and was believed to have been influenced by the Cavendish expeditions, not least in the description of St Helena, which became the land base for the moon expedition. (Francis Godwin died in April, 1633, and is believed to be buried at his former residence in Whitbourne in north-east Herefordshire, although no stone marks his grave).

A more recent memorial can be found at the northern end of the graveyard, beyond the church if you're approaching from the main lychgate. In 2003, underneath the trees and near the bench, Reverend Jimmy Morrison unveiled a plaque in memory of all of the former patients of St Mary's Hospital in Burghill who lie in unmarked graves. The hospital, now an upmarket housing estate, served many purposes during its time, including as a mental asylum. Many of the former patients were buried without any records. The ground has now been conse-crated.

BURRINGTON

The small village of Burrington is believed to date back to Domesday and the pretty church of St George's dates from around 1864, although there have been churches at the same site for hundreds of years before then. The rebuilding in 1864 was financed by the Boughton Knight family from nearby Downton Castle and it's the graves of the Knight, Hare and Walker families that are of partic-ular interest.

An iron grave slab at Burrington

The eight cast iron grave slabs were originally inside the church but are now visible on the raised platform at the end of the church, immediately on the right of the path as you enter the graveyard. Although slabs such as these can be seen elsewhere in the country these are very early examples, dating from 1619, and unusual in Herefordshire. The lettering changes from the sans serif style of the 17th century to the full serif style of the 18th century. They are remarkably well preserved and were most probably cast in the nearby furnaces at Bridgnorth, owned by the Knight family who were at the centre of iron production in the area from Elizabethan times. During my two visits tiny pieces of tartan cloth were visible tucked under each stone, maybe a talisman to a distant relative?

CASTLE FROME

St Michael's Church is Norman and was probably built around 1125 by a member of the de Lacy family who arrived in the village following the Norman conquest. It contains the Unett Tomb in the chancel which is believed to contain the last remains of William Unett and his wife Margaret who died in the early 17th century. The effigies are shown on top of a tomb chest which contains images of nine children in fabulous detail. The four girls and five boys are believed to be the de Lacy children.

William Unett is shown as a cavalier and is pictured in full

Effigies of William and Margaret Unett at Castle Frome

22

dress, with the folds of fabric on his sleeves and trousers, his boots and his flamboyant moustache and tiny beard shown in amazing detail. His wife is equally detailed and her feet are the only part of the effigy to be damaged. Both are holding bibles and their heads rest on dark green coloured pillows.

The nave also contains a basic stone slab carved in memory of the same William Unett, 'former High Sheriff and Justice of the Peace' who died on 22 August 1624. The memorial was carved by his second wife Anne. The church also contains a memorial to Francis Unett (1656) and Sara Unett (1659).

Opposite the Unett tomb is a tiny but remarkable memorial to an unknown man. The carved stone knight can be seen at the base of the south-east chancel window and shows him in chain mail holding his

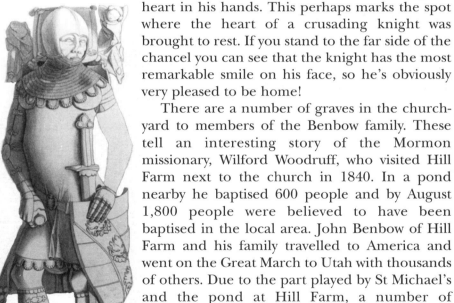

heart in his hands. This perhaps marks the spot where the heart of a crusading knight was brought to rest. If you stand to the far side of the chancel you can see that the knight has the most remarkable smile on his face, so he's obviously very pleased to be home!

There are a number of graves in the church-yard to members of the Benbow family. These tell an interesting story of the Mormon missionary, Wilford Woodruff, who visited Hill Farm next to the church in 1840. In a pond nearby he baptised 600 people and by August 1,800 people were believed to have been baptised in the local area. John Benbow of Hill Farm and his family travelled to America and went on the Great March to Utah with thousands of others. Due to the part played by St Michael's and the pond at Hill Farm, a number of Americans visit each year.

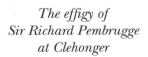

*The effigy of
Sir Richard Pembrugge
at Clehonger*

CLEHONGER

All Saints Church, Clehonger, contains a very impressive effigy to Sir Richard Pembrugge who founded the chantry chapel in 1341 and died in 1346. Sir Richard is shown in full armour dated by experts as being from 1336 to 1340, has his sword on his left side and holds his shield on his left hip.

The coat of arms on the
shield contains three detailed gargoyle-like
figures aligned in a vertical row, all of which are
sticking their tongues out! His right hand also holds a
small, short-handled dagger. Sir Richard's head is resting on a
cushion supported by two angels, one of which is badly damaged,
and has a dog at his feet. The tomb now stands on the edge of St
Anne's Chapel and the nave which is believed to be its original position, but before 1956 it was placed at the east end of the chapel. Some
of the original colour can still be seen on the tomb chest and the statue
of the dog.

In the opposite corner of the side chapel is a very small effigy, only
four feet in length, of Sir Richard's wife, Petronilla, who is believed to
have died in 1348, two years after her husband. The couple had three
children: Sir Richard Pembrugge who was one of the first Knights of the
Garter under King Edward III, Hawisia and Amicia. Petronilla is
portrayed in a tight fitting gown and a mantle with her head resting on
a cushion supported by angels. At her feet is an unusual bird which has
seized the folds of her gown in its beak. The parish notes believe that the
bird is a stormy petrel, known in Italian as a Petrello, which may have
been used as a pun on her name.

Alongside the effigy of Petronilla are the Barre Brasses. The two
figures have been mounted on a specifically designed wooden board to
protect them and prevent corrosion; originally they were in a stone
slab on the floor of the chapel. The brasses show Sir John Barre who
helped to found the
chantry and died in
1482 or 1483. He is
portrayed wearing
armour from the late
15th century and his
head rests on a tilted
helmet with his feet
resting on a lion. The
other figure portrays
his second wife Joan,
the widow of a Robert
Greyndour, who died
in 1484. She is wearing
a low cut dress from
the period, and a late
15th-century butterfly

Detail from the Barre Brasses

headdress, whilst a small acorn is attached to the girdle around her waist. At her feet are resting two dogs.

The Barre family took over the manor of Clehonger from the Pembrugges when Sir Thomas de la Barre, grandfather of Sir John Barre, married Hawisia, the daughter of Sir Richard and Petronilla. The shields also contained on the wooden display board are believed to be from a branch of the Pembrugge family and may not actually belong to the Barre Brasses.

The graveyard also contains a number of interesting memorials. As you leave the porch, straight ahead are two large stones to the Taylor family who lived at the Valletts. The first stone is in memory of Thomas Taylor who died at the age of 20 on 17 July 1813 after being clubbed on the head by a work colleague. Thomas was a groom for Colonel Matthews at Belmont House and he shared a room with the coachman. One evening after a late night out he arrived back to find the door locked and tried to wake the coachman, but couldn't rouse him. Thomas then forced the door open but unfortunately the coachman mistook him for an intruder and struck him over the head with a club. He died a few days later and the coachman was found guilty of wilful murder by a coroner's jury, but later the charge was reduced to manslaughter by the Assizes Court. According to parish records he was fined one shilling and given a month's imprisonment. The unusual story is recorded on Thomas's gravestone:

> This young man whose character was in every respect excellent ... [this part cannot be read] ... his Death from an unfortunate blow given in a moment of anger by a fellow servant. His loss was deeply lamented by his inconsolable parents and friends and much regretted by his family at Belmont where he lived and by ever person who knew him.

The bad luck continued in the Taylor family as the adjoining headstone records the deaths of Thomas's three brothers just two years later. John Taylor aged 32, William Taylor aged 27 and James Taylor aged 25 died in 1815 as their inscription details:

> Where by the sinking of a boat, in which they were returning from their daily labours, were unfortunately drowned in the River Wye on the evening of the 10th of March 1815, leaving three widows and ten helpless children to the protection of that providence whose Mercy extends over all His Works, but whose ways are inscrutable to Man.

Just to the right of the Taylor stones is a headstone which marks the deaths of three members of the Phillips family who were all blacksmiths in Clehonger. Although the stone has become quite difficult to read, it is in memory of John Phillips who died in 1771, James Phillips who died in 1850 and Thomas Phillips who died in 1859. A line from the poem *The Cuttar's Sunday Night* is carved on the bottom of the stone: 'An honest man's the noblest work of God'.

A few steps north from the Phillips' stone, directly in line with the tree, there is a cross in memory of Private Benjamin Preece who was a member of the 1st Dragoon Guards. Private Preece lived a few miles away at Haywood and fought at the battle of Waterloo. He died in 1870 at the age of 87 and, if you move the grass at the bottom of the stone to one side, you can still make out the word 'Waterloo' carved at the base of the cross.

In the graveyard there is an example of the many memorials to children who were not baptised and are therefore buried outside the churchyard walls. To the right of All Saints behind a group of trees and a hedge is a grave to Margaret Rose Holmes who was born on 8 January 1935 and died on 2 December 1944 aged nine. Why her grave is located away from the main graves is just supposition, but very poignantly it is a very well tended grave despite being situated next to a modern sign saying 'Plastic and paper only in bin'.

CLIFFORD

St Mary's Clifford is an ancient church, believed to have been built by the monks of the former Clifford Priory in the 13th century, although 19th-century work has altered the church's appearance greatly. The church contains one of only two wooden effigies in Herefordshire; the other can be seen at St Bartholomew's, Much Marcle. The effigy is contained in an alcove in the chancel and is believed to date from the 12th century. It clearly shows a priest in Eucharistic vestments, and histo-

The wooden effigy at Clifford

rians believe it could
either represent a previous vicar of the parish
or one of the Cluniac monks from the former priory.

Local legend says that the effigy actually represents the founder of the priory and that it was brought to St Mary's during the Dissolution in the 16th century. Records show that the effigy was carried around the churchyard in a procession on founder's day and that it was always carried into the church before funeral processions.

CLODOCK

The Church of Saint Clydowg, situated at the foot of the Black Mountains, is itself a monument. Legend states that Prince Clydowg, son of the 5th-century King Clodwyn of Ewias, was murdered by a rival in love one day as he was out hunting. When his body was being transported for burial on an ox-cart, the yoke broke whilst crossing the River Monnow and the oxen refused to go any further. This was taken as a sign that Clydowg should be buried by the river and, as pilgrims subsequently travelled to his tomb, he was sanctified and a church was built at the spot. The mainly Norman church, which is what we see today, was built on the same spot but a fragment of a much earlier stone church can be seen inside.

Clodock and nearby Longtown became well known in the late 19th century due to the case of the 'Longtown Harrier'. On 12 January 1893 William Prosser of Hunthouse Cottage in Longtown was set upon by six men who rolled him in snow and chased him through the village. He tried to hide but was captured and thrown in the River Monnow. He vainly tried to run for help but couldn't raise anybody and so fled again across the snow-covered fields. He was found the next morning hanging by his clothes which had caught on a cottage gate; he had frozen to death. The six men claimed it was a prank which had gone tragically wrong but they were tried for manslaughter in Hereford on 3 March 1893. All pleaded guilty, but were given light sentences for being generally of good character, with the longest sentence being one year in prison.

William Prosser is buried in Clodock Churchyard and his grave can be seen by the wall on the right of the graveyard as you enter through the lychgate. Situated next to the second sign about 50 metres along is a stone on which most of the writing is indecipherable. It is, however, possible to make out the name William Prosser and the date 1893.

COLWALL

The large church of St James the Great stands in the original Colwall village, about half a mile away from the more populated current village centre. It contains numerous wall tablets and memorials to the families who owned the rich surrounding estates in centuries past, including the Brydges, Brights and Lamberts. On the wall of the south aisle is a remarkably well preserved brass in memory of Elizabeth Harford. The detailed engraving is in memory of the wife of Anthony Harford, a gentleman from Bosbury, who died on 19 July 1590. She is shown facing her husband in full period dress; he is in armour with a sword at his side. Their six sons and four daughters are also shown either side of her with the younger boys in the feminine dresses commonly worn by young gentlemen at that time. There also three shields bearing coats of arms at the top of the brass and the detail of the line work is remarkable. The brass has been copied in order to preserve the original.

There are numerous memorials to the Lambert family on the walls of the north aisle, including Jane Lambert and Catherine Lambert who were successively the wives of Henry Lambert of nearby Barton Court. Sarah Lambert, who lived at Barton Court in the 18th and 19th centuries is buried alongside her family at Colwall Church although it's now impossible to pinpoint her exact grave. She was the heiress of Barton Court but rejected her family by eloping with a young man. Unfortunately he turned out to be a fraud and, having been tricked out of most of her possessions, she had to return home with just her wedding ring remaining. The poet Elizabeth Barrett Browning, who lived at nearby Hope End as a child, later wrote about the unfortunate Sarah Lambert, whose ghost is rumoured to haunt Barton Court and the nearby Barton Holloway.

CROFT

St Michael and All Angels at Croft stands in the grounds of Croft Castle. Although the castle is owned and run by the National Trust, you are able to access the church by a path alongside the main drive. It's worth the visit as the small church contains a remarkably detailed tomb chest to Sir Richard (d.1509) and Dame Eleanor Croft (d.1520). The stone tomb shows Sir Richard in armour with his feet resting on the Croft lion and a jousting helmet under his head. Dame Eleanor is shown with similar lions and a dog at her feet and angels surround her head. Unusually, the effigies portray the couple in old age. The tomb itself is flanked by shield bearers and at their heads is an amazing carved canopy showing the figures of St Sitha, St Margaret, St Anthony and St Riche. He fought on the Yorkist side at the Battle of Mortimer's Cross in 1461 and the Battle of Tewkesbury ten years later and is believed to be portrayed in the armour in which he fought at Tewkesbury. Sir Richard held a range of post during his lifetime—Sheriff of Herefordshire from 1471 to 1472 and 1477 to 1486, MP for Herefordshire in 1477, Treasurer to King Henry VII, and also served as Governor of Ludlow Castle.

Dame Eleanor was the widow of Sir Hugh Mortimer of Kyre and the daughter of Sir Edward Cornewall, Baron of Burford. She had been in charge of the Royal Household for the sons of Edward IV when they lived at Ludlow Castle and who were subsequently murdered, it is thought on the orders of Richard III. Her first husband, Sir Hugh Mortimer, is buried in Martley Church in Worcestershire where his effigy can be seen.

The chancel also contains monuments to Sir Herbert Archer Croft who was killed at Gallipoli in August 1915. He was the tenth Baronet and was born on 5 September 1868. Alongside is the memorial to James Herbert Croft, a Captain in Number One Commando squadron and the eleventh Baronet and only son of Sir Herbert. He was killed on active service on 15 August 1941.

The tomb of Sir Richard and Lady Eleanor Croft

The small churchyard at St Michael and All Angels contains tablets, stones and graves to members of the Croft and Scudamore Croft families, and also a tiny square stone in the corner of the graveyard by the footpath to 'Rufus Bourke' who was born on 9 September and died on 15 November 1976 'much loved'.

CUSOP

The churchyard at St Mary's Cusop close to Hay-on-Wye is the final resting place of two people with equally tragic and remarkable stories to tell.

William Seward was born in Badsey in Worcestershire in 1702 and died in Cusop in 1740. During his short life he gained an international reputation as a Methodist preacher. William went to London as a young man and made his fortune through business and soon became a generous benefactor to the poor of the City. It was a meeting in 1738 with the Reverend Charles Wesley that changed his life, and he soon became closely involved with the early Methodist teachers and their evangelical works. William soon began to travel on preaching tours at home and abroad and on his return from a trip to America in 1740 he began an open air preaching tour of his own. He encountered hostile crowds throughout south Wales and at Hay-on-Wye in October of that year he was stoned by an aggressive mob, and a few days later he died of his wounds, becoming the first Methodist martyr.

The top of the gravestone to William Seward, and tablet in the church (below)

He is buried in Cusop churchyard, under a yew tree on the south-east side of the church, and in 1978, 238 years after his death a memorial tablet was erected to him inside the church. It contains the following inscription in both English and Welsh:

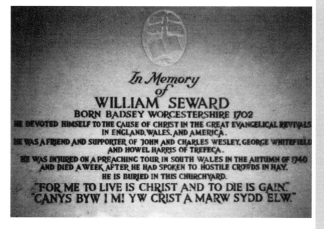

In Memory
of
WILLIAM SEWARD
BORN BADSEY WORCESTERSHIRE 1702
HE DEVOTED HIMSELF TO THE CAUSE OF CHRIST IN THE GREAT EVANGELICAL REVIVALS
IN ENGLAND, WALES, AND AMERICA.
HE WAS A FRIEND AND SUPPORTER OF JOHN AND CHARLES WESLEY, GEORGE WHITEFIELD
AND HOWEL HARRIS OF TREFECA.
HE WAS INJURED ON A PREACHING TOUR IN SOUTH WALES IN THE AUTUMN OF 1740
AND DIED A WEEK AFTER HE HAD SPOKEN TO HOSTILE CROWDS IN HAY.
HE IS BURIED IN THIS CHURCHYARD.
"FOR ME TO LIVE IS CHRIST AND TO DIE IS GAIN."
"CANYS BYW I MI YW CRIST A MARW SYDD ELW."

For me to live is Christ and to die is gain
Canys byw I mi yw Crist a marw sydd elw

Cusop churchyard also contains the remains of Margaret Armstrong who has become far better known in death than she was during her lifetime. Mrs Armstrong died on 22 February 1921 and was buried at St Mary's, but before too long her body was being exhumed after her husband was accused of her murder. Herbert Rowse Armstrong was a solicitor who originally hailed from Newton Abbott in Devon. His wife was believed to have died from arsenic poisoning and the finger pointed at the well known figure in Hay-on-Wye society. In due course he was found guilty of her murder and eventually hung at Gloucester Jail on 31 May 1922. The case made national news as Armstrong had personally acted for the mother of John Lee, a convicted murderer who was eventually released in 1907. In recent years many theories have been put forward to suggest that Armstrong himself may have been set up and was innocent of any involvement in his wife's death; these are best explained in Martin Beales' book *The Hay Poisoner*.

DEWSALL

The tiny country church of Dewsall contains a very unusual modern memorial depicting two gravestones linked together. It commemorates Michael John Murrican, an American, who was killed in a road accident on 28 May 1977 aged just 24. He was due to marry a young lady from Dewsall Court the following day and had been travelling to Herefordshire for his wedding. His fiancée still regularly visits the churchyard.

DINEDOR

St Andrew's Church in Dinedor is a tiny church nestling behind a farm in the small village. Inside it contains a brass cross in memory of Bertie Davies, the son of Edward and Emma Davies, who died on 8 June 1906 'after bravely rescuing two comrades from drowning in the Wye'.

Fragments of a much older gravestone are on display in the window of the church's bell tower. Marking the grave of one William Bull it is possible to just make out most of a poem inscribed on the stone:

Remember man, as you pass
As thou art now, so once was I
As I am now, you will be
Therefore ...

31

DORMINGTON

St Peter's Church, Dormington, is beautifully preserved and contains a rather ugly but very rare gargoyle doorknocker, stop and have a look as you enter inside the church! Inside are two monuments at which it's worth taking a closer look. On the wall immediately opposite the door is a wall table to John Brydges who died in 1669. Although few details of John Brydges's life are provided, he is remembered with this poetic inscription:

Blest soule, whose happy mansion is above
In that quire where they only sing and live
If Saints view humane actions, thou shalt see
A griefe as great as thy loved memory
Divided thus, I'll mourne till heaven prove just
and once more match my body to the dust.

Just to the right of the Brydges wall tablet is a touching memorial to Catherine Atwood who died in 1855 aged 83. For 59 years she was the 'attached friend' of the children of Edward and Eliza Foley of the nearby manor of Stoke Edith Park.

DORSTONE

St Faith's Church at Dorstone is believed to have been founded by Richard de Brito and his descendants in an act of penance. Richard de Brito was one of the four knights who murdered Thomas à Becket in 1171 and, after completing 15 years of penance in the Holy Land, he settled in Dorstone. The earliest records state that the de Brito family added a chapel dedicated to the Virgin Mary to an earlier structure on the site of St Faith's. The medieval church was demolished in 1827 and its replacement likewise in 1889. When the present church was then built some remnants of the medieval church were found and re-utilised. The location of the grave of Richard de Brito is unknown but a tomb believed to be that of his descendant, Johannes de Brito were found under the south wall.

EASTNOR

The Church of St John at Eastnor is closely linked to Eastnor Castle and contains many monuments to members of the Cocks and Somers family who were the estate's landowners for several generations. The Cocks family held the seat since the 16th century and then enlarged the estate by marrying into the Somers family, rich landowners from Worcestershire. However, the most interesting grave in the village is not contained in the church or the churchyard, however. As you approach Eastnor from either Colwall or Ledbury you will see an obelisk on the Malvern Hills high above the settlement. This was built in 1812 by the first Earl Somers, Charles Cocks, in memory of his eldest son who was killed whilst serving under Wellington during the siege of Burgos during the Peninsular War. The church was not rebuilt until 1852 and, as the work on the present castle only began in 1812, maybe the earl wanted a lasting memorial to his son that could be seen from every part of the new estate?

Memorial to Edward, the eldest son of Lord Somers, killed in the Peninsular War, and other family members

EATON BISHOP

St Michael's Church, Eaton Bishop, contains a well-documented memorial tablet in the chancel to Richard and Margaret Sneade who died within a few months of each other in 1678. Translated, the tablet reads:

> One bed we shared; one tomb now holds us,
> And our bones, mingled with dust now lie together.
> One death was ours; one year took us away,
> One day saved us and gave us back to God.

A relative, Richard Sneade, who died in 1714, is remembered with a memorial and is described as an 'honest man who never thought ill to any person'. The church also contains a brass to the Revd. Charles Burroughs, who helped to raise the money for the elaborate church organ which was built in 1888 and restored in 1984, and an alabaster memorial to Lady Pulley, the wife of Sir Charles Pulley of nearby Lower Eaton, who died in January 1942.

Near the tower arch you can see an example of a very early monumental stone. Incised with a cross, chalice and book, the stone is thought to have originally covered the grave of a former parish priest, although no exact details are known.

EDWYN RALPH

The small parish church at St Michael and All Angels contains a host of intriguing memorials that lead to even more intriguing stories. Lying under the tower are six stone effigies of varying ages, all preserved in great detail.

The oldest, of a man and wife, are believed to date from 1290. The man has his legs crossed, his head is resting on two cushions and his feet on a lion and a dog. He holds a large shield on his left arm decorated with a coat of arms which the church guide book believes are the arms of the Zedeffen family. His wife is shown with her hands in prayer and a small dog at her feet. The carving leaves her with a very peaceful expression on her face.

At their feet lie another four effigies, perhaps the most interesting of which is that of either a child or a very small woman which is placed between the two groups of adults and is an exact miniature of the older figures. The figure has her feet resting on a dog and her hands clasped in prayer.

The second set of effigies may be dated slightly later than the first and show a knight lying alongside two women. The knight is again shown in armour with his feet lying on a dog and a lion and he is also holding a shield on his side. The two female figures are both shown smiling serenely, with their hands in prayer and dogs resting at their feet.

The larger shield obviously suggest that the effigies are members of the Zedefen family most probably Radulfus de Zedefen, Lord of Yedefen, and his son, Thomas de Zedefen. The village is believed to have taken the second part of its name from Radulfus and the family played a major role in the history of the area. Radulfus last served in a military capacity in 1282 and died in 1296, whilst Thomas was knighted in 1306 and died in 1329. His son Thomas (Radulphus's grandson) is believed to have died during the Black Plague in 1348, and local historians believe that the female effigies may refer to Radulfus's daughters rather than Thomas's wife. They may also have died during the plague, although it is impossible to verify this.

The true history of the effigies may not be as romantic and interesting as the folklore which suggests that the figures are actually the Lord Edvin and Baron Ralph who gave their names to the village. The two friends are alleged to have fallen in love with the same woman and to have duelled for her hand in marriage at a nearby bridge. The lady whose love had caused the fight threw herself between the men in order to stop the duel and was mortally wounded. For centuries visitors to the area have been told that the effigies show the two rival knights now lying alongside each other in death—a romantic tale indeed.

The group of effigies at Edwyn Ralph

Alongside the stone effigies is an incised slab in memory of Maud de Edefin—the wife of Sir Thomas de Edefin, most probably the same Sir Thomas referred to above with a different spelling of his surname. She is shown wearing a sleeveless dress and a very formal wimple, suggesting that she probably outlived her husband. The Latin inscription is the only example of a pardon monument in the county and reads:

Here lies the lady Maud; she was the wife of Sir Thomas de Edefin. To whomsoever shall say a Pater and an Ave for the soul of Maud de Edefin the Lord Bishop of Worcester will allow thirty days of pardon, and the Lord Bishop of Hereford sixty days of pardon.

Whatever Lady Maud did to receive such an honour isn't documented, but she must have lived a very worthy life to have been rewarded in such a manner by the two adjoining bishops.

The effigies and the slab were originally in the tomb recesses in the chancel before being grouped together in their present position under the tower. Alongside them on the tower wall is a stone tablet in memory of members of the Burwall family from nearby Butterley which gives an insight into the social history of the time. The 8-feet tall tablet is engraved with hops and two angels or cherubs at the top, and the remains of gold paint can also still be seen. The engraving reads as if generations of the family were added gradually but also shows how low the average life expectancy was for some during the 17th and 18th centuries. Anne Burwall, her husband, Thomas, and son, Edward, all died in 1699, Anne in August and Thomas and Edward in November; suggesting maybe a time when illness was sweeping through the parish? Thomas and Mary's other son, also a Thomas, died in January 1727 predeceased by his daughter, Mary, who died in November 1714 and followed by a second daughter Jane who died in July 1732. His son, another Thomas, died in June 1737 aged 21, another daughter, Elizabeth, in January 1749 aged 26 and another son, John, in March 1744 aged 21. There is no mention of the death of Thomas's wife, also called Mary, and additional children although the line must have continued as the memorial also refers to Peggy Burwall who died in 1835 aged 70, and the church chalice was donated by a Mrs Burwall in 1800.

EYE

St Peter and St Paul at Eye is a hidden gem of a church tucked away down a small lane. The north chapel contains a number of effigies, all wonderfully preserved, including one in alabaster which is believed to be that of either Sir Thomas Cornewall (1444–1500) or Sir Rowland Cornewall (d.1520) who lived at nearby Berrington Hall. It shows a knight in armour and chain mail with much detail on his collar and cross and gauntlets lying at his side. His face and hair are especially well preserved. His feet are shown resting on the red Cornewall family lion, and images of animal paws are also shown on his helmet.

The second tomb in the north chapel shows Sir Richard Cornewall, son of Sir Thomas, and his wife. The alabaster effigies show a knight in formal dress with a chain around his neck, sword at his side and his feet on the Cornewall lion. The detail on his wife's hair and face is very well

preserved and the tomb
chest shows seven children and three angels,
presumably those that died in infancy, around the
sides.

Between the two tombs is a memorial pilaster on the wall of the north chapel which was designed by Sir Reginald Bloomfield. It remembers the three sons of Lord and Lady Cawley of Berrington Hall who died in the Great War. Major John Stephen Cawley died on 1 September 1914 at Nery in France aged 34, Captain Harold Thomas Cawley on 24 September1914 at Gallipoli aged 37 and Captain Oswald Cawley on 22 August 1918 near Merville aged 35.

There is also a wall plaque to Thomas Harley, the son of the third Earl of Oxford, who was Lord Mayor of London, the MP for Herefordshire for 25 years and who moved to Eye Manor at the end of his life. He died at the manor and is buried in the churchyard.

The north aisle contains two very unusual wall brasses to two members of the Carver family. The top brass shows an angel with its wings forming a heart and is in memory of Louisa Drinkwater Carver (1880–1949) a 'dear sister'. The second brass is in the shape of a wreath with a woman wearing a loose dress and praying in the centre of the wreath. This is dedicated to Marjorie Aspinall Carver and appears to have been crafted by Ernest Gillick.

The south aisle has a window and brasses in memory of Wilfrid and Catherine Buckle and their grandson Edward Adrian Buckle West who died in 1934 aged 17. Wilfrid Buckle (10 February 1854–12 April 1935) was the vicar at Eye for 37 years.

It's also worth spending time in the well maintained churchyard, where there are a number of modern wall plaques to members of the Sandford and Spicer families, and also a touching gravestone to Jane and Elizabeth Philips. This stone, which has an engraving of two clasped hands, is in memory of Elizabeth Philips who died on 9 June 1858 aged 9 and her sister Jane Philips who died on 10 October 1903 also aged 9.

*Effigy of
Sir Rowland Cornewall*

EYWAS HAROLD

Eywas Harold has an intriguing and interesting history.
The former settlement of Ewias had a castle which was held
in the reign of Henry I by Harold of Ewias who gave his name to
the village. He went on to found Dore Abbey where he is buried.
The present church of St Michael's has been on its present site since
the 13th century but there would have been religious buildings in the
area for many years before that. The most interesting feature of the
church is the stone effigy of a woman which lies in a tomb recess on the
north wall of the chancel. It's believed to portray Clarissa Tregoz, the
daughter of John Tregoz, Lord of Ewias, and the great, great granddaughter of the original Harold of Ewias.

Clarissa was the granddaughter of Juliana, the sister of Thomas de
Cantilupe, and her grandfather, Robert de Ewias,
died at the battle of Evesham fighting
for de Montfort's army in 1265.
Her father, John Tregoz,
renewed links between the
family and the Crown and was
a Constable of the Tower and
Guardian of London for
Edward I. He died in 1300
and it's believed that
Clarissa, his eldest daughter,
died before him. She was
married to Roger de la
Warr and their son John
took over the castle and
the lordship, although he
wasn't thought to have
spent much time in the
area.

Despite being dated
to the later 13th
century the effigy is
still amazingly
detailed and shows a
young woman with
her head on a pillow
and a dog or a lion at
her feet. She is

The effigy of Clarissa Tregoz

38

wearing a long, folded
gown, an elaborate head-dress which covers
her neck and her chin, and is holding her heart in her
long and graceful fingers. She has an enigmatic smile and a
distinctive snubbed nose, and is shown with her eyes closed. The
church guidebook tells the interesting story of the Reverend Fowle
who investigated the effigy in 1865 and found a cavity under her hands
which contained the remains of a metal vessel lined with fabric in which
he was certain her heart had been deposited.

GOODRICH

St Giles Church, Goodrich, contains a rather unusual choice of gravestone by a former vicar of the parish. J.B. Herbert died on 17 March
1863 and, according to his wishes, an enormous boulder was dragged by
traction engine from Doward Hill to the churchyard. The parish records
show it was so large that part of the surrounding wall had to be demolished to gain entry. The boulder is not easily missed and can be found
on the village side of the churchyard, halfway along the side of the
church. The inscription on the plaque reads: 'Let not the strong man
glory in his strength'.

HAY-ON-WYE

The modern graveyard at Hay-on-Wye sits just on the boundary between
England and Wales and contains a remarkable memorial to Lancelot
Steele Dixon. If you take the main path through the cemetery the grave
is just on the right as the path reaches a T-junction.

Lancelot Steele Dixon was the son of Christine Dixon, an accom-
plished sculptress and the second wife of the novelist Rafael Sabatini.
Christine was the sister-in-law of Sabatini's first wife, Ruth Goad Dixon,
the daughter of the Liverpool paper merchant
Lancelot Steele Dixon (senior).

The story of Lancelot's
death is horrific. On
the day that

*The memorial to Lancelot
Steele Dixon at Hay*

he gained his RAF wings
Lancelot (known as Lanty) decided to fly over
the home of his mother and step-father at The Clock
Mill, Winforton, near Hay. His mother and Rafael watched
from the garden as he flew overhead but then something went
terribly wrong with the flight and he crashed in a nearby field, dying
as his plane burst into flames.

Christine (Dixon) Sabatini's monument to her son is both beautiful
and moving. It shows an angel lying on the grave as if he is asleep. The
detail on the brass is remarkable and the inscription reads:

Pro Patricia
Pilot Officer Lancelot Steele Dixon – RAF.
Killed at Winforton 9th April 1940 in the 24th year of his age.
Mater Luctuosa Facit

HEREFORD – ALL SAINTS

All Saints Church in the centre of Hereford now contains a lively vegetarian café which has brought life back into the building. It is still in use as a church as well and contains wall tablets remembering some of the past parishioners.

In the lady chapel there is a tablet to the family of Captain Thomas Bennett and his wife Sarah who sadly lost two of their children in 1835. Their son, Edward Watkins Bennett was a 'Mastershipman of his Majesty's Ship *Rainbow* who died at Port Royal, Jamaica on July 31st 1835 aged 19 – a victim to the malignant fever of that country.' His sister Sarah died on 31 October 1835 aged 16 'after a long protracted illness.' Their parents, who lived at Broomy Hill, both long outlived them. Captain Bennett died in June 1870 aged 86 and his wife in September 1876 aged 84.

All Saints also contains a brass memorial to David Garrick who was 'born in this parish and baptised in this church'. The former Herefordian was born on 28 February 1716 and died on 20 January 1779—he is interred at Westminster Abbey. Garrick, who is also listed as having been born a year later in 1717, is one of Hereford's most famous sons and was hailed during his lifetime as being one of the greatest British actors. He made his name in 1743 after his outstanding performance as Shakespeare's Richard III and went on to become a highly successful theatre manager. Garrick is credited for bringing a new sense of realism to the British stage and was a co-owner of the Drury Lane theatre until his retirement, when he sold his share to the playwright Sheridan.

HEREFORD – CATHEDRAL

The cathedral contains a wealth of interesting monuments and memorials, and there are a number which stand out from the rest for either historical reasons or because of their originality. In the north transept is the tomb of Thomas Cantilupe, Bishop of Hereford from 1275 to 1282 and canonised as St Thomas of Hereford in 1320. Hereford became a place of pilgrimage following his death with his tomb worshipped as a shrine. After being born in Buckinghamshire in 1218, Thomas was educated by his uncle, Walter Cantilupe, bishop of Worcester, before continuing his education at Oxford and Paris and soon gained a reputation as an ecclesiastical scholar. He became Chancellor of Oxford University in 1262 and was appointed Chancellor of the Realm in 1265. It is generally thought that he was not keen to accept his appointment as bishop of Hereford and would have preferred to stay in London rather than take up the troubled post on the English/Welsh border.

St Thomas soon found himself involved in the feudal wars of the Marches but gained a name as a man who would always defend the help-

The shrine to St Thomas Cantilupe

less. He stood up against the arrogant ways of many landowners, including Gilbert de Clare, the Red Earl of Gloucester, and Lord Clifford. Before his death in 1282, St Thomas was involved in a lengthy dispute with John Peckham, archbishop of Canterbury, who eventually excommunicated him. St Thomas then travelled to Rome to see Pope Martin IV who eventually gave him absolution just hours before his death at Ferento near Montefiascone.

His chaplain, Richard Swinefield, who became the next bishop of Hereford, had travelled with him to Italy and at St Thomas's request had the saint's body boiled to separate his flesh from his bones. The former was interred at a church in Italy, his heart was buried in Ashridge in Buckinghamshire and his bones were brought back and interred in Hereford Cathedral. Apparently a number of strange happenings and 'miracles' then occurred, including that the bones started to bleed again when they were touched by Gilbert de Clare, earl of Gloucester, who had wronged St Thomas in life. After prayers were said at his tomb, speech and hearing was said to have been restored in people, lepers were cured and dozens of people apparently were restored to life. His shrine was extensively restored in 1999.

Amongst the other memorials in the north transept is a brass to the two sons of James Atlay, bishop of Hereford from 1868 to 1894. Reverend George William Atlay went to Africa as a

The tomb of John Swinefield—showing the play on his name in the carving of the pigs on the arches

missionary but was violently murdered by a band of 'marauding savages' near the shores of Lake Nyasa on 26 August1895 aged 28. His brother, Charles Cecil Atlay, also died in Africa after being wounded whilst fighting on Wagon Hill, Ladysmith, on 6 January 1900. He eventually died from his injuries at Durban on 28 March.

The tomb of John Swinefield, Precentor at the cathedral from 1294 to 1311 and the nephew of Bishop Richard Swinefield who succeeded Thomas Cantilupe, is highly unusual and original as it is surrounded by carvings of pigs feeding on acorns! The tomb recess is by the steps of the lady chapel and is painted in blue and gold. The reason for the animal adornment is believed to be a pun on his name.

Another unusual tomb chest can be found in the crypt. Andrew Jones, who died in 1497, and his wife are buried alongside each other by the entrance to the crypt, and his effigy shows amazing detail. It's immediately obvious that his feet rest alongside a barrel of cider, highlighting his career as a reputed cider maker. He was also a generous bene-factor to the cathedral during his lifetime.

In the south transept the tomb slabs to Bishop Herbert Croft who died in 1691 and Dean George Benson who died in 1692 lie alongside each other, and the stonemasons have assured their special friend-ship is never forgotten as their hands are carved clasped together across the individual tomb slabs. Bishop Croft, who is believed to have been buried underneath the Bishop's Throne, carried on preaching despite the presence of the Roundhead soldiers during the Civil War who rampaged through the cathedral, looting and vandalising the treasures and monuments. Bishop Croft insisted that the service went ahead as normal and despite having guns levelled at him he used his sermon to condemn the actions of the soldiers. He was only saved due to the intervention of the Roundhead Commander Colonel Birch (for whom see the entry for St Peter and St Paul at Weobley).

The poet John Phillips is also commemorated in Hereford Cathedral. As the author of the poem Cyder, *his brass includes a sprig from an apple tree*

HEREFORD –
ST MARTIN'S

Although one of the city's most modern churches, St Martin's is well known across the world as the last resting place for members of the Special Air Service. Although the elite regiment have now moved

from their former base at Stirling Lines, just past the church, their former members are still buried at St Martin's. The S.A.S. graves are situated next to the wall at the back of the church and are easily iden- tifiable due to their distinct white stones and grey wall tablets. The graves date from 1974 through to 2004, a reminder that conflict is constantly taking place across the world. Many of the men died during the Falklands war and more recent deaths have taken place in Afghanistan and during the first Iraq war.

St Martin's showing a line of S.A.S. memorials

HEREFORD – ST PAUL'S

St Paul's, Hereford, contains the last resting places of many former sons of the city. The family of the artist Brian Hatton, are buried here although he himself is remembered on the war memorial at St Nicholas's Church.

At the right-hand end of the church as you approach from Church Lane is a grave in memory of two young brothers who drowned in the nearby River Lugg. The stone marks the grave of John Francis Lionel Money-Kyrle (aged 14) and George Staunton Money-Kyrle (aged 11) who lived at Aylestone Hill. The inscription tells how they drowned in the Lugg on 18 June 1863, 'the elder giving his life in nobly attempting to save his younger brother. They were lovely and pleasant in their lives and in death they are not divided. The care of them is with the most high.'

HEREFORD –

ST PETER'S

Most Herefordians walk past the grave of one of the city's most eminent Victorians on a daily basis without a clue as to the history that lies beneath their feet. The churchyard of the old St Peter's Church is now used as a walkway between Commercial Road and Canal Street and sadly is often littered with the results of many of the nearby fast-food restaurants. In the middle of the site, just off the main path, is a large grave surrounded by iron railings and it is here that the Reverend John Venn M.A. is buried. Rev. John Venn did an amazing amount for Hereford. He established the Hereford City Mission, the 'Society for Aiding the Industrious' which still exists, and set up the city's allotments, public baths, a dispensary, soup kitchens, alms-houses, a corn mill and, in a very forward-thinking manner, a credit union. The street on which the mill stands was originally known as Brookside, but the name was renamed Bath Street late in the 19th century, as the steam from the mill (now Berrows House) was used to heat the public baths which were housed behind it. The old baths building is now a Masonic lodge.

The name John Venn is also widely known in mathematical circles as Reverend Venn's nephew, also John Venn, invented the Venn diagram statistical model.

Despite the numerous legacies that Reverend Venn left the city, his gravestone is incredibly modest with his inscription merely saying: 'John Venn M.A. Sometime vicar of St Peter's and St Owen's. Died May 12th 1890 aged 1890.'

He is buried alongside his sister Emelia Venn whose inscription is more detailed: 'Emelia Venn – daughter of Reverend John Venn – Rector of Clapham and sister of John Venn M.A. Died 25th Feb 1881 aged 87. At her own request the following verse is inscribed on her tomb 'Thy statutes have been my songs in the house of my pilgrimage'.

Also buried in the same plot is a second relative, Jane Catherine Venn: 'Daughter of the late Rev Henry Venn, died 19th July 1853 in the 93rd year of her Age'. Her last words were 'It is finished. Hear the dying saviour cry'.

The gates leading to the graveyard contain a memorial stone to Reverend Venn which provides more details of his life:

Rev John Venn M.A.
Vicar of this Parish 1833 – 1870, fell asleep May 12th 1890, Laid to rest in this burial ground. One of Hereford's greatest benefactors.

Founder   of
The Hereford Society for Aiding the
Industrious 1841, Hereford City Mission 1856,
A friend and a guide to the poor. His sister Emelia
Venn was associated with him in his good work.
By love serve eachother.

HOLME LACY

St Cuthbert's Church, Holme Lacy, has not been in regular use since 1994 but is still consecrated and is cared for by The Churches Conservation Trust. It stands almost a mile and a half from the village, at the end of a long lane, overlooking the River Wye. St Cuthbert's

contains a collection of beautiful and impressive monuments, the majority to members of the Scudamore family, former residents of Holme Lacy House and Lords of the Manor.

In the chancel is a tomb chest with alabaster effigies of John Scudamore who died in 1571 and his wife, Sibell Vaughan of Hergest near Kington, whose relatives are described in more detail in the entry for St Mary's, Kington. The effigies are very detailed and show John in armour with his sword at his side and his feet resting on a lion. Sir John was a former High Sheriff of Hereford and an usher to King Henry VIII.

On the north wall is a monument in white and grey marble to James Scudamore (grandson of John and Sibell) who died in 1668. He was knighted for bravery at the siege of Cadiz and is believed to have been the Sir Scudamore described by the poet Edmund Spenser in his poem

The effigies of John Scudamore (d.1571) and Sibell Vaughan

The Fairie Queen in 1596.

The poem filled three volumes and told an epic story of chivalric romance. Spenser used a new metre which he had invented for the poem and which is now known as the Spenserian stanza. He described James as 'Sir Scudamore, pattern of chivalry'. On his effigy he is shown leaning on his left elbow facing an obelisk which is situated next to his memorial and commemorates his wife Jane Scudamore.

Their grandson, John Scudamore, is commemorated by a monument on the south wall of the south chapel containing a sarcophagus, a flaming urn, two skulls and two cherubs. John Scudamore died in 1716 at the age of just 33.

The south chapel contains numerous other monuments to members of the Scudamore family whilst the nine vaults beneath the church contain the remains of many generations of the family. Of particular

Memorial to James Scudamore who died in 1668; the memorial itself is later

The effigy of John Scudamore, Viscount Sligo, who died in 1716

The cherubs opposite are from the tomb of Jane Scudamore who died in 1699 aged 71

interest is the monument to Chandos Scudamore-Stanhope, a Captain in the Royal Navy who died on *HMS Caledonia* in 1871. His monument shows an angel rising from a rock alongside an anchor and a fleet of ships.

The churchyard also contains a number of very impressive memorials. If you go out of the porch and turn left you will find a small gate in the south-east corner which is enclosed by yew hedges. Although the burial plot has become quite overgrown one figure can be clearly seen: a life-sized bronze monument to Edwyn Francis Scudamore-Stanhope, 10th earl of Chesterfield, who died in 1933. He was a Knight of the Garter and is portrayed in his armour, holding his shield and with his dog lying at his feet, looking out along the meadows to the River Wye. A large wrought iron gate, believed to have been moved from Holme Lacy House, stands in front of him and features the family crest and motto.

The life-sized bronze monument to Edwyn Francis Scudamore-Stanhope in the churchyard

HOLMER

Saint Bartholomew's Church in Holmer is now situated just off the A49 on the northern edge of Hereford and was once the parish church of a very prosperous hamlet. The nave contains a wonderfully well-preserved wooden wall tablet to Jane Howarth who died in 1652. The oak tablet features pictures of a skull and crossbones, a sand timer at the top and this marvellously descriptive inscription:

An epitaph on the death of Y virtuous gentlewoman Mrs Jane Howarth the wife of Richard Howarth esq who deceased the 5th day of November 1652.

Here age and virtue lyes, and who could have
Two fairer partners, buried in a grave
Her age decayd, her virtue cannot be,
Consum'd, but breath's unto Eternitie

Mirror of patience, void of homebred strife
A civil matron and loyal wife
Rest then in peace Sweet Soule, for thou wert even
A Saint on earth and now a Saint in Heaven

She's gone before us, in peace let her sleep
Until wee overtake her, let us weepe.

The remains of tomb slabs to the Howarth and Caldicott families originally lay on the church floor but were removed in the church restoration of 1860. However, they can now be seen in the porch alongside a thick stone coffin lid believed to be from the 13th century.

There is also a brass near the altar to the Reverend Francis Henry Tuke, MA who was vicar of Holmer from 1908 until 1916 and a chaplain to the forces from 1914 to 1916, 'Who was killed in France near Bernafay Wood whilst carrying water to his men in the trenches who were suffering from agonising thirst.'

The gravestone of Mary Croom, with the hand emerging from the top of the stone showing the inscription

The churchyard contains a number of unusual tombstones including an intriguing lead panel set into a rough stone in memory of Elizabeth Godsall (d.1856) and William Godsall (d.1871). Just to the right of the porch as you leave the church and on the left of the path which leads to the back of the vicarage is also an unusual stone cross set on a pile of carved stones. Look closely and you can see a carved human hand emerging from the stones. The gravestone marks the last resting place of Mary Croom who died in 1873 and, unsurprisingly, the rather creepy and unusual sight is full of fascination for many children from the nearby school!

One gravestone which has never been found is that belonging to Mrs Oliver who is believed to have died in 1884. The Oliver family lived at the nearby Turvey Hall and were parishioners of Holmer Church. Mrs Oliver

suddenly disappeared to
be never seen again, and local rumour says that
she was murdered by her husband and buried in the
grounds of the Hall. Although there are records of the
deaths and burials of all other members of the Oliver family, her
whereabouts remain a mystery!

HOPE-UNDER-DINMORE

The church of St Mary the Virgin at Hope-under-Dinmore contains a
rather special monument which is unfortunately tucked away from the
gaze of the majority of the congregation. The huge marble memorial
to the Earl and Countess Conyngsby is situated in the side chapel and
is believed to be dated to the mid-18th century, although no inscriptions are visible. Made of white and grey marble
and standing approximately 20 to 25 foot high, it
is believed to be the work of the sculptor
Roubiliac but this hasn't been confirmed by
documentation.

The statue shows the earl and
countess in formal dress and she nurses
their infant son on her knee; the child is
believed to have choked to death on a
cherry stone in 1708. The detail on
the statues is remarkable, with facial
details and the earl's head of ringlets
amazingly brought to life.

The side chapel also contains a
marble tablet which has been moved
and mounted on the wall. It shows a
man and his wife surrounded by their
family of three sons and four daughters. He is shown in armour and both
he and his wife have their hands
clasped in prayer. Sadly the inscription around the edge of the tablet is
illegible.

Tucked away in the vestry,
originally the north transept, is
an unusual very tall and thin
The statue believed to be of the Countess marble stone plaque in
Conyngsby and her son by Roubiliac memory of John Arkright of

50

Hampton Court (1785–1852) and his wife Sarah (1808–1869). It stands about 8 feet tall and contains a brass inlay. John Arkright inherited the family fortune made in the cotton spinning business and took over Hampton Court from the Conyngsby family in the early 19th century. The transept also contains a brass memorial to their son, Henry Arkright, who died in an avalanche whilst climbing Mont Blanc in 1857. His body was not discovered until 1897 and is buried at Chamonix.

In front of the main church door is also a good example of a wooden wall memorial. The painted plaque is in memory of 'Robert Whitehall, a Gentleman from Penin' who died on 3 August 1789 aged 68. The colours on the plaque are still very vivid and it's easy to make out two cherubs at the bottom complete with crowns and trumpets and the family shield at the top of the plaque.

IVINGTON

St John's Churchyard in the small village of Ivington just outside Leominster is not the most obvious resting place for European royalty, but it contains a grave to Princess Sophia Mickeladze. The Russian princess is believed to have been related to the former Romanovs, and she fled her homeland in 1917 as a refugee. Although she arrived in Herefordshire to live at Bankfield House in Ivington, her husband Prince Iverico was imprisoned in Russia and they were never reunited. Her husband died in 1931 and the Princess eventually gained permission to bring his body to Britain. She eventually died in 1943 and they are buried together just to the left of the porch.

The grave is marked with a Russian Orthodox stone cross and a simple inscription, but the *Hereford Times* reported in February 2005 that children from Ivington Primary School had studied the story for a history project and were trying to persuade the parish council to erect a more fitting memorial for a royal couple.

KENCHURCH

The church of St Mary the Virgin at Kenchurch lies at the end of the drive to Kenchurch Court, home of the Scudamore family and one of the estates in the country that has been longest lived in by members of the same family down the generations. The real treasure contained in the church is the tomb of John Scudamore who died in 1616 aged 37 and his wife Amy, the daughter of John Starkie of Chester. It is tucked away in an alcove just off the chancel and consists of a tomb chest and many individual wall panels and small statues. John Scudamore is portrayed in alabaster and is shown in full armour with his sword at his side and holding a bible. His wife, who erected the monument, and his nine children are portrayed in stone, with Amy Scudamore lying alongside her husband and wearing a ruff and a widow's veil.

Sadly much damage was done to the monument when the church was broken into in 1972. The miniature figures of the nine children were damaged and two of their heads removed. Subsequently the figures were rather crudely cemented on to the surrounds of the tomb but the detail is still very clear. All of the children show individual expressions and the youngest but one child is shown holding a skull, whilst their infant child is shown in a cradle.

There are many wall tablets throughout the church in memory of other members of the Scudamore family, including Lucy Scudamore who died four days after giving birth in 1798 and the son to whom she gave birth, who subsequently took the name John Lucy Scudamore. The churchyard also contains many large crosses in memory of members of the family. The floor of the chantry used to contain a number of tiles containing brass Scudamore family shields but the shields were prised

The monument to John and Amy Scudamore and their nine children

out and stolen. As a
result the church is kept locked, although the
key is available at the School House.

St Mary's is also rumoured to be the last resting place of
the famous border character Jack O'Kent. The mythical man,
sometimes also described as the devil, features in many stories
passed down through the generations. Indeed there was a vicar called
Jack Kent who served the parish in the late 14th century, and who is
portrayed as a wild-eyed man in a painting still held at Kenchurch
Court! Jack O'Kent was believed to be buried half in and half out of the
walls of St Mary's but as no remains were found when the church was
rebuilt in 1859, I think the story can be considered just a local myth!

KINGSLAND

The large church of St Michael and All Angels at Kingsland contains a
memorial plaque to members of the Gethin family whose sad deaths are
part of a remarkable tale. Mr Gethin had an architect's practice in
Cardiff but the family home was just outside Kingsland. The wall tablet
in the chancel remembers John Gethin aged 30, Emily Gethin 25 and
their children Lorna 4, John 2, their nurse Eliza Preston and their friend
Jemima Peace. The party had all gone to Africa in September 1895 to
spent time in a better climate to help improve Mrs Gethin's weak health.
They were returning home on board the steamship *Drummond Castle*,
owned by the Castle Mail Packet Company, which had sailed from Cape
Town on 28 May 1896 bound for London via Las Palmas. The voyage had
gone well and on the evening of 16 June the ship was approaching
Ouessant, an island just off the Brittany coastline. Most of the passengers
were celebrating the next day's homecoming and had only just retired
to their cabins at 11 o'clock when the ship ploughed into rocks. She took
just three minutes to go down and only three men survived from the 246
people on board: Quartermaster Charles Wood, Seaman William
Godbolt and a first class passenger, Charles Marquarat. The bodies were
gradually washed ashore and recovered by the residents of Breton, the
small town in which they were subsequently buried. The wreck of the
steamship was not discovered until 1979 where it was found some 200
feet down, where it remains.

Near the church door there is a small and touching stone in memory
of Joan Greenaway who died on 19 October 1683 aged 5 years. The
inscription must have been read by hundreds of parishioners as they
leave the church:

So young and so soone
dead, conclude we may,
Shee was to Goode longer on, Earth to stay.

Attached to the porch is the small Volka Chapel which is believed to have been built originally as a chantry in which masses were said for the soul of an early benefactor of the church and the village. There are no conclusive records of when or for whom the chapel was built, but it is generally thought that it was for a member of the Mortimer family who paid for the first priest in Kingsland in 1285. Prayers for the many men lost as the nearby battle of Mortimer's Cross in February 1461 were also said in the Volka Chapel. It contains an enclosed stone tomb chest under an ornate arch which would have been made for a man of approximately 5 feet 8 inches tall.

KINGS PYON

The church of St Mary's at Kings Pyon stands in the middle of a small group of farm buildings and houses, but the legacy of one family buried nearby is now known throughout the world.

In 1720 Richard Tomkins of nearby New House wrote his will leaving to his second son, Richard, a yoke of oxen named Spark and Merchant, and to his fourth son, Benjamin, who was born in 1714, the 'cow Silver and her calf'. Benjamin used the bull calf to breed with two cows, Pidgeon and Mottle, which

The Volka Chapel, Kingsland

he also inherited from
his father, and the records of their ongoing
breeding plan led to the publication of the *First Herd
Book of Hereford Cattle* in 1846 by Thomas Eyton of Wellington
in Shropshire. From 1886 onwards, Herd Book entries have been
confined to only those cattle whose sire and dam have ben recorded
in previous volumes. There are three Richard Tomkins buried in the
churchyard, the first who died in 1790 is most likely to be the second
son, and the subsequent generations of men named Richard Tomkins
are probably his descendants. You can clearly read the inscriptions for
Richard, son of Richard and Anne, who died in June 1807, and Richard
who died in 1818.

Benjamin Tomkins moved from Kings Pyon to farm in Canon Pyon
and then Wellington and during the next half a century he changed the
breed from a plough ox into the beef cattle with which we are familiar
today. Documents show that the breed was already widely known for its
dark red or brown colour with white faces. The breed progressed during
the next two centuries, and through careful breeding became the
gorgeous looking stocky beasts that Herefordshire is famous for
throughout the world.

The Tomkins family are also remembered through numerous wall
tablets in the church, including those in the nave of George Tomkins
who died in June 1854 aged 79, his wife, Elizabeth, who died in
September 1822 aged 49 and their infant son, George, who died in 1800
aged just five months. In the chancel there are wall tablets to Benjamin
Tomkins who died in October 1815 aged 71, most probably Benjamin
Junior, and his wife, Sarah, who died in July 1819 aged 72. The family
links continue through the mentions of their first three daughters:
Sarah who died in 1838 aged 64, Mary who died in 1851 aged 73 and
Elizabeth who died in 1855 aged 74. The family continued through the
fourth daughter Margaret who married William Cooke, and their relatives are buried in the churchyard and remembered through a series of
wall memorials.

St Mary's also contains two interesting effigies now housed in the side
chapel. The alabaster effigy of a knight is quite badly damaged and he has
lost his legs and arms, but the remaining torso and head are in a good
state of repair. He is shown wearing armour including a bascinet and his
head is resting on two cushions with a very detailed carved lion at his feet.
The lion itself is portrayed either wearing chain mail or with a very sturdy
and warlike long main. The knight's lips are very interesting as they are
pursed as if he is about to kiss an imaginary beau, or maybe he is calling
the many visitors to show their respects with an embrace?!

Lying next to him is a
stone effigy of a lady wearing a detailed head
dress with angels lying at her head and a dog resting at
her feet. She is believed to be a member of the Mortimer
family and the effigy is thought to date from the mid-14th
century. Both lie on a tomb chest with seven canopies detailed on
the front, and you can still make out glimpses of colour on the chest
and on both effigies.

KINGTON

St Mary's, Kington, sits on a hill overlooking the border market town. Inside the church lie the mortal remains of two former residents of Hergest Court and clues to one of the area's most famous folk tales. The magnificent alabaster and marble tomb of Thomas and Ellen Vaughan can be seen in the side chapel, immediately to your right as you enter the church. The tomb is surrounded by figures of saints and angels on all four sides and features elaborate effigies of Thomas and Ellen. The effigies are highly detailed although unfortunately there has been some damage to Lady Vaughan's feet and to the dog lying at the feet of Thomas Vaughan. The craftsmanship shown on Lady Vaughan's hands and her husband's chain mail and boots are worth close attention.

The effigies of Ellen and
Thomas Vaughan

The tomb itself is well worth a visit, but it's the story behind Kington's most famous residents that ignites the imagination.

Thomas Vaughan was a 15th-century lord who was killed at the Battle of Banbury in 1469 whilst supporting the Yorkist cause. Tradition says he was an incredibly evil man, although the lack of documentary evidence backing this up leads many to believe his nickname of 'Black Vaughan' may well be attributable to his black hair rather than his demeanour. According to local legend, after his headless body was brought back and buried in Kington, Black Vaughan was a restless spirit who wreaked havoc amongst the townsfolk after his death by appearing in many forms, namely as a fly which tormented horses, a dog, and a huge black bull that entered the church. Eventually 12 local clergymen were summoned to lay the spirit. Despite encountering difficulties during the ceremony, they are alleged to have shrunken the spirit of Vaughan, sealed it in a snuff box and buried it beneath a large stone in the bottom of Hergest Pool. Like all folklore, the amount of fact contained in the story is difficult to assess but the power of the Vaughan legend lives on, and a visitor to the church in recent times witnessed a bull like apparition form in the air. Ironically, the visitor was a distant relative of Thomas Vaughan!

Lady Ellen Gethin, wife of Thomas, also has an intriguing tale to tell. Known as 'Ellen The Terrible' it seems her nickname may have been just as exaggerated as her husband's as again records point to her being a good and honourable woman. One moment marked her reputation in death as in life though, as she exacted retribution for the death of her brother. David Gethin had been murdered at Llanbister by a man called John Hir whom some documents record as a cousin of the Gethins. Ellen decided to seek revenge on behalf of her brother and, disguised as a man, she entered a nearby archery contest. As John Hir aimed at the target, Ellen shot her brother's murderer at point blank range.

The Vaughan's legacy continues with the story of the black dog of Hergest Court, a companion to Thomas Vaughan which is believed to have had its own room at the top of the house. The dog is said to have haunted generations of the Vaughan family ever since, appearing before them to signify imminent death. It's widely thought that Sir Arthur Conan Doyle based his Sherlock Holmes story *The Hound of the Baskervilles* on the tales of the black dog and, as he did stay at Hergest Court and had heard of the nearby Baskerville family from Eardisley, maybe the story is based on fact. The people of Dartmoor in Devon aren't too keen on Herefordshire's attempts to claim their famous tale though!

KINNERSLEY

St James Church in Kinnersley stands next to Kinnersley Castle and unsurprisingly the two buildings are closely linked. The interior of the church contains a fabulous example of the wall painting of Anglican church designer George Bodley, who had an enormous influence on church design in the latter stages of the 19th century. He married Minna Reavely in 1872 and, as her family lived at the castle, it came as no real shock that he joined forces with the new rector, Frederick Andrews, in 1873 and together they re-designed the interior and organ case at St James. Reverend Andrews' grave, marked by a large Celtic cross, can be found alongside George Bodley's in the churchyard. Reverend Andrews died on 16 April 1920 and George Bodley died in 1907 at the age of 80.

The church also contains a large monument to the former Lord of Kinnersley and Letton, Francis Smallman, who died in 1635, and his wife Susan. They are shown kneeling and praying, facing each other under a very detailed canopy held aloft by

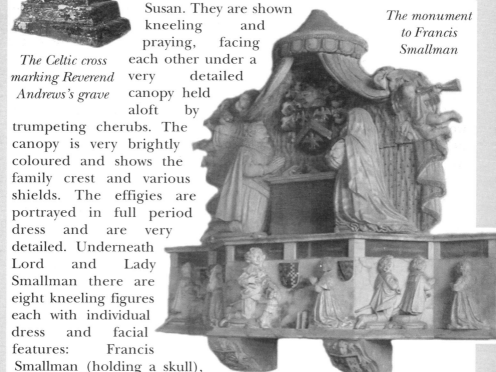

The Celtic cross marking Reverend Andrews's grave

The monument to Francis Smallman

trumpeting cherubs. The canopy is very brightly coloured and shows the family crest and various shields. The effigies are portrayed in full period dress and are very detailed. Underneath Lord and Lady Smallman there are eight kneeling figures each with individual dress and facial features: Francis Smallman (holding a skull),

Jane Smallman, Ione Smallman, William Smallman and Alfie Smallman, plus John Clarke, William Clarke and Susan Clarke.

Directly below the monument is a brass to William Leviot, a former rector of Kinnersley, who died in 1421 and thus lived at the time of Henry V. He is shown praying in his priest's robes with a very stern face.

KNILL

The tiny parish church of St Michael's in the hamlet of Knill contains the grave of Sir Samuel Romilly and his wife, Lady Anne Romilly, the daughter of Francis Garbett of the neighbouring Knill Court. Sir Samuel was born in London in 1757, the son of a wealthy jeweller, and went on to become a noted student and lawyer. He entered Parliament and soon gained a reputation for his humanitarian reforms, as he fought for many worthy causes such as the repeal of the death penalty for small offences such as pick-pocketing, the end of flogging as a military punishment, for the humane slaughter of animals and the emancipation of slaves. In 1806, whilst working as solicitor general in the cabinet of Lord Grenville, he commenced work on laws that would improve bankruptcy practice and, although he didn't live to see major changes in his lifetime, his proposals were adopted during the following decades and still form the backbone of many of today's laws. He became a member of the Queen's Counsel and a knight.

Despite his illustrious working life, Sir Samuel was a family man and worshipped his wife Lady Anne. When, in 1818, she became seriously ill and died on 29 October aged 44 he was devastated and was so overwhelmed by grief that he killed himself three days later, aged 61. Lady Romilly's funeral was postponed and they were buried together at Knill church. A memorial tablet to the couple can be seen inside the church alongside many other dedications to members of Lady Romilly's family.

LEDBURY

St Michael and All Angels at Ledbury is one of the biggest in the county, and worth a long visit. It contains some of Herefordshire's most beautiful effigies, giving excellent examples of sculpture through the centuries. One of the most interesting is a marble memorial to John Hamilton Martin, a baby who died in 1851 and is shown with angels watching over him.

Although it's known that the memorial was made by Thomas and Mary Thornycroft who also made sculptures of Queen Victoria's children, very little documentation exists on John Hamilton Martin himself. His brief life is a mystery but the memorial can be seen in the chancel of the church.

His grandmother Penelope had inherited the Upper Hall estate in Ledbury from her father John Skyppe in 1812 and the family lived in the house until 1921, when it changed hands and became a mixed grammar school.

The sanctuary contains a fabulous monument to Edward and Elizabeth Skynner shown kneeling and facing each other with portrayals of their ten children kneeling beneath them. Edward, who died in 1631, was a wealthy man involved in the cloth trade but perhaps more interesting is the baby girl detailed lying between them. According to local legend, their daughter was killed by the last wolf in the district. The central figure amongst the sons is William, a former chancellor of the diocese, who is shown wearing his ceremonial robes. It was he who erected the monument to his parents.

The Skynners were part of the select group of inter-related families who owned and controlled most of Ledbury and the surrounding estates in the 16th century. Edward Skynner was responsible for the construction of New House, described at one point as 'the grandest black and white house in this country'. In 1585 the house was sold to the Biddulph family (see later).

The memorial to John Hamilton Martin

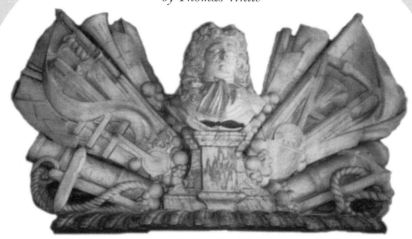

*Part of the memorial to
Captain Samuel Skynner (d.1725)
by Thomas White*

The south chapel contains an alabaster slab memorial to Canon Edward Cooper, a former Archdeacon of Hereford and master of St Katherine's Hospital in Ledbury, who died in 1596. St Katherine's was built by Hugh Foliot in 1231 to provide spiritual and material well-being for the poor, sick and distressed pilgrims and travellers. By the 15th century the masters of the hospital were living in the Mansion House next door rather than in the common dormitory. This was part of an attempt to restore some order and structure to the hospital. Canon Cooper was master of St Katherine's from 1562 until his death and enjoyed a decent standard of living and a high place in the social hierarchy of Ledbury.

On the east wall is also a carved monument to Daniel Saunders (died 1825) which shows a man leaning on his staff with his dog at his feet. Next to him are shown his wife and infant child.

The most visually striking memorials inside the church are found in the south aisle. The Biddulph family lived in Ledbury Park and the family tomb is on the raised area in the corner of the aisle. The memorials include one to Anthony (d.1718) and Constance (d.1706) Biddulph who are shown reclining with their feet facing towards each other; a woman sitting under a weeping tree which is in memory of Michael Biddulph (d.1800) and a marble figure of a mourning woman in memory of Robert Biddulph (d.1814). Constance was the daughter and co-heiress of Francis Hall who had owned Ledbury Park and the New Hall estate and passed it over to his daughter on her marriage to Anthony Biddulph in 1688. The Biddulph family also founded the Cocks, Biddulph bank in 1757 which was dealing until it was taken over

by Martins Bank in 1919.
The firm later went on to form part of Barclays
Bank. It was through the links between the Cocks,
Biddulph and Martins banking businesses that James Martin
II married Penelope Skyppe and through their descendants the
Upper Hall estate passed to John Martin III (see the earlier refer-
ence to the Martin memorial). The two banking dynasties played a
major role in the affairs of Ledbury town for many decades.

The vestry contains a 14th-century altar tomb showing the effigy of a
lady with her robes draping over the edge of the tomb. She is believed
to be a member of the Grymbald Pauncefoot family (see the entry for
Much Cowarne). Also contained in the vestry is a monument to Mr and
Mrs Moulton Barrett, the parents of the poet Elizabeth Barrett
Browning. The family lived at Hope End, Ledbury, for many years until
the death of Elizabeth's mother.

One of St Michael and All Angels most simple tombs is also one of its
most important. In a niche in the baptistry (also known as St Katharine's
Chapel) is an effigy of a Benedictine monk, believed to date from the
13th century. The baptistry is thought to have been originally intended
for use as a chapter house as it is square-shaped and has none of the
provisions or details associated with a sanctuary. The effigy is thought to
have been used as a coffin lid originally, and was found buried under the
floor during the 19th-century restorations of the church.

During my research for this book, the churchwardens were painstak-
ingly noting the details of the many floor tablets throughout the church
before the inscriptions become indecipherable. Their notes, which are
available in a leaflet for sale in the church, are worth studying as they
give us a vivid picture of life in Ledbury in the past as most of the graves
note the occupation of the deceased.

One of the most interesting graves is contained in the
churchyard. As you approach from Church Lane,
follow the path around to the right of the church and
a quarter of the way up the side wall on the right you
will find a line of six tombstones. Fourth from
the left is that of Thomas
Russell, a former
Blacksmith of

Anthony Biddulph

62

Ledbury, who died on 24 May 1838 aged 46 years. His grave contains this charming poem which is decaying rapidly but can still just be read:

> My sledge and hammer lie reclined
> My Bellows too have lost their wind
> My fire's extinct my forge decayed
> And in the dust my vice is laid
> My Goal is Spent, My Iron gone.
> My nails are drove my work is done.
> My fire-dried corpse now lies at rest.
> My soul smoke-like is soaring to the blest.

Constance Biddulph

63

LEINTWARDINE

The Church of St Mary Magdalene's most detailed monument lies hidden, but if you enter the vestry via the organ steps then you'll find the marble memorial to Sir Banastre Tarleton. The large memorial depicts a battle scene with armour and plumed helmet, bible scroll, sword and flag and remembers a rather colourful character who died on 15 January 1833 aged 78. The detailed inscription is a story in itself:

This monument is erected to his memory by his bereaved widow as a testimony of her affection. But he has raised a more imperishable memorial for himself in the annals of his country and in the hearts of many friends.

> He was a Hero! His youth's idol, Glory.
> He courted on the battle-field, and Won!
>
> England exulted in her valiant son,
> And stamp'd his name for ever in her story.
>
> Time's trophy gain'd and sheath'd the warriors sword
> He turn'd him sated from the world renown,
> To die the humble soldier of his lord
> And change Earth's laurel for a heavenly crown!

The memorial lists some of Tarleton's many positions and honours including General in the army, Knight Grand Cross of the order of Bath, Baronet, Governor of Berwick-upon-Tweed, Colonel of the 8th Hussars and Liverpool MP for seven years, but his life was even more colourful that the memorial suggests.

Born on 21 August 1754, Tarleton was a second son and joined the dragoon guards in 1775 after spending his fortune socialising in London. He spent five years fighting in the American War of Independence and was a distinguished soldier but he also got into great debt through gambling in America. He was thought to be an unorthodox soldier, but he was mentioned in Cornwallis's dispatches to the king and arrived in England in January 1782 as a hero. His portrait was painted by Reynolds and Gainsborough although Gainsborough later destroyed the painting as Tarleton hadn't paid for it! The remaining Reynolds painting, which portrays Tarleton with a missing finger, hangs prominently in the National Portrait Gallery.

A friend of the Prince of Wales, he partied and gambled in London and started a relationship with Mary 'Perdita' Robinson, a famous actress and poet. He was forced to move to France after accumulating more debts and stayed abroad whilst his family, friends and Cornwallis paid off his creditors. He eventually became MP for Liverpool and in 1798 he quickly married Susan Priscilla Bertie, the illegitimate daughter of Robert Bertie, Duke of Ancaster. He also fathered an illegitimate daughter born to a Russian immigrant called Kolina. The daughter, Banina, was born in 1801 but died aged 17.

Tarleton moved to Leintwardine in 1814 and in 1816 he requested and was granted a Baronetcy. Rather ironically, his coat of arms read 'after clouds – sunshine'. Tarleton took part in the coronation parade of King George IV in 1820 before spending his last years in north Herefordshire. In recent years Tarleton has found fame again as the character Colonel William Tavington in Mel Gibson's film *The Patriot*, which is based on his story. Perhaps Tarleton's greatest claim lies in his book which suggests that he could have kept the United States as a British colony had he been properly supported by Lord Cornwallis!

Tarleton's Memorial

I had much help from local residents in trying to pinpoint the exact grave of Sir Banastre but it still remains a mystery. There are two theories. It is believed that he could lie under the platform built in the chancel as the Victorians broke up many coffin slabs in the nave and chancel during their restoration of the church in 1864. Another thought is that the large iron casing at the northern end of the churchyard surrounds his grave, the markings and inscriptions of which cannot be read. The grave was once surrounded by iron railings but these were removed during the Second World War.

LINTON

St Mary's, Linton, may be able to claim to be the only church which holds a memorial to a former vicar who died jumping from a stagecoach. This unusual death was met by the Reverend Arthur Matthews who apparently sustained injuries whilst abandoning a stagecoach after the horse that was pulling it took fright. He died on 23 September 1840 aged 52 and there is a marble tablet memorial to him and his wife Elizabeth under the tower. Reverend Matthews was a canon of Hereford Cathedral and was the vicar of Linton for 28 years.

The base of the tower also contains a memorial to William Matthews and his wife Jane and to the Reverend Peter Senhouse who was the vicar of Linton for 57 years until he died in 1760 aged 90. If you search amongst the tables and chairs that are stored there you will see a number of stone coffin lids. One square lid with a tailed cross has been identified in parish records as possibly belonging to a heart burial in 1150. There is also a 13th-century stone lid showing a head and shoulders, a lid showing a double cross which has been dated as 13th century, a slab showing a cross and eagles believed to date back to the 14th century and a simple slab with a cross detail which may be dated as far back at 1150.

LITTLE DEWCHURCH

The churchyard of St David's at Little Dewchurch contains a number of unusual gravestones with tales to tell. As you enter from the bottom gate there is a white military stone to the left marking the grave of Guardsman P. Drinkwater of the Grenadier Guards. The story behind the new stone is a triumph for community spirit. Guardsman Drinkwater died in 1919 and a stone was erected but many, many years later parishioners noticed that the memorial inside the church gave him his full title '11183 Guardsman P. Drinkwater MM' but the 'MM' was missed off his headstone. They contacted the War Graves Commission who inspected the stone and found it was too small to contain the alteration so a new stone was made in France from the traditional creamy white Caen stone used for military gravestones and brought to Little Dewchurch more than 80 years after his death.

As you continue up the path and pass the church you will come across a grave marking the final resting place of another local man who lost his life fighting for our country. A large cross marks the grave of Walter Dallow who was a member of the 2nd Battalion South Wales Borderers

and who died on 18
April 1917 aged 29. Walter was wounded in the
battle of Arras but survived and was placed on board a
hospital ship bound for home. Tragically the ship was torpe-
doed and although Walter survived and was plucked from the
water, the exposure had proved to be too great and he died the next
day. His gravestone contains a carving of crossed pistols and his regi-
mental helmet.

If you turn and walk up the hill with the church to your left you will
come across an ordinary looking plot marked by a low square wall.
According to its owner this is the last resting place of the 'true King of
England'. Anthony Hall was born in London in 1898 and claimed that
he was a direct descendant of the illegitimate son of King Henry VIII and
Anne Boleyn who was born before he divorced Katharine of Aragon.
Hall was a member of the police force but he became a wealthy man
after inheriting his father's fortune and subsequently devoted his life to
addressing public meetings and attempting to convince people of his
claim. He also wrote to King George V in 1931 branding him an
imposter! Hall died in December 1947 at the age of 49 and, despite wide
fame during his lifetime, it's unlikely that many of the visitors to St
David's are aware that they may well be passing by a royal grave.

LITTLE HEREFORD

The church of St Mary Magdalen at Little Hereford contains the most
intriguing mystery that I have come across when compiling this book. As
you enter the church, turn immediately right and on the side wall alongside the porch door is a stone tablet in memory of 16 children of the
parish who died in the summer of 1870. Although the inscription is
starting to disappear at the bottom, the majority can be clearly read:

> Suffer little children to come unto me and
> forbid them not: For of such is the kingdom
> of God and he took them up in his arms, put
> his hands upon them and blessed them.
>
> James Bennett aged 5 years
> Annie Bennett aged 12 years
> Thomas Child aged 14 months
> Mary Ann Child aged 5 years
> Caroline Edith Clifton aged 10 weeks
> Edward Cook aged 4 years

Jane Edwards aged 3 years
Edwyn Edwards aged 20 months
Emily Griffiths aged 18 months
Rose Ellen Hall aged 5 months
Walter Price aged 4 years
Edward Rowberry aged $9^3/4$ years
Alice Watts aged 7 years
Mary Watts aged 4 years
John Watts aged 6 years
Harriet Watts aged 8 years

All of this parish when su [the rest cannot be read] in the summer of 1870.

None of the children listed are buried in marked graves in the churchyard and none of the parishioners have any knowledge of why and how they died. There are some tiny iron crosses in the churchyard immediately on the right as you enter through the gate, maybe they hold the answer?

The graves of two men who may be the fathers of some of the children listed can be seen in the churchyard. Leonard Clifton who died on 24 May 1876 aged 39, 'for ten years station master at Easton Court Station', and William Cook who died on 11 June 1920 aged 70. The vicar at the time of the children's deaths was W.M. Tomkins whose grave can be seen just to the right of the main path. He died on 24 January 1874 aged 73 and was in charge of St Mary Magdalen from 1844 to his death.

Despite many hours spent searching through the county archives there is still absolutely no clues as to how, why and where the children died and where they are buried. The parish records show numerous children born and baptised between 1856 and 1868 who share the surnames of the dead youngsters but not one of them is listed. Perhaps more importantly, there are only six burials listed from 1870 onwards and just two of these were recorded by Reverend Tomkins. The other four deaths and additional parish happenings were recorded by the curate H.M. Burrows. His record keeping is random to say the least and nowhere near as organised as that of Reverend Tomkins. Perhaps the vicar was absent at the time of the deaths? Clues to the location of some of the children's homes can perhaps be found in the 1881 census which lists a number of families bearing some of the surnames shown on the monument.

There are three families of Edwards listed in the census: Evan Edwards, a labourer, and his three daughters and son lived at Little Hereford Crossing; Ann Edwards, a farmer's widow, and her son Francis lived at Broadfield House; and Samuel Edwards, a slate layer, and his

wife, Eliza, a washer-
woman, lived at Park Villas. There are two families in the parish with the name Cook; William, a farm
labourer, and his wife Mary and two sons lived at Park Villas.
His daughter, Mary Anne, is listed as a scholar whilst his sons
were a slate layer and a farm servant. The residence of William
Cook, another farm labourer, and his wife, Anna, and daughter,
Elizabeth, cannot be read clearly. William Rowberry was a turnpike
labourer in 1881 and together with his wife Elizabeth, a laundress, they
lived at Bradley Cottage. John Watts, a labourer, and his wife, Sarah, and
two sons, all farm servants, also lived at Park Villas whilst David Price, a
farmer, and his wife, Rose, lived at The Cliffs in 1881. Stuart Hall is listed
as a tailor and, although we know he lived with his wife Mary and three
sons, the place of their residence cannot be clearly read. Could these be
the families of the children who died so tragically in 1870?

The church also contains a wall monument to Sir Joseph Bailey of
Easton Court which shows a woman praying. He died on 31 August 1856
aged 54 and was MP for Herefordshire. The court was a Georgian house
when Sir Joseph bought it in 1837 but he added a number of contrasting
extensions which didn't prove too popular. The court was damaged by
fire in the 1950s and is now mostly derelict. There are also floor slabs to
members of the Peake family and three brass plaques near the altar. The
chancel also contains a marble plaque to Frances Martha Gough who
died as an infant, and which contains this verse:

> Ere sun could blast or sorrow fade
> Death came with friendly care
> Transferr'd the flower to the skies
> And bade it blossom there.

LLANDINABO

The tiny church of St Dinabo (the only church dedicated to him in the
entire country) is situated on private land at Llandinabo Court, but
access is easily gained by calling at the farm office for the key. The
church is no bigger than a terraced house, but the chancel contains a
very interesting brass memorial to Thomas Tompkins. Thomas drowned
in May 1629 and the brass shows a detailed picture of him standing in a
pool of water. Thomas is, unsurprisingly, looking very solemn and there
is a lengthy inscription in Latin beneath him. The church also contains
a stone coffin lid on display near the altar and, for a very small parish, a
remarkable number of graves in such a tiny churchyard.

LUGWARDINE

St Peter's Church at Lugwardine contains a memorial tablet to William Reed, a former resident of New Court, the estate on the edge of the village looking towards Hereford. He's shown in his Cavalier dress reclining on one side. His family are still remembered in the village courtesy of an old folk tale, numerously re-told and passed down through the generations. William, who died in 1634, was the son of Gabriel Reed who had moved to New Court from Bronsil Castle at Eastnor. Gabriel was troubled and haunted by what he believed to be a restless spirit so he took advice and was told to somehow obtain a few bones from the tomb of a Lord Beauchamp, a former resident at Bronsil Castle. Folklore says that the spirit then stopped troubling Gabriel Reed, but so determined was he that the haunting wouldn't happen again that he brought the bones with him when the family moved to Lugwardine. Although the exact whereabouts of the bones isn't known, they are believed to be contained somewhere in New Court or its grounds.

Most of the tombstones in the churchyard cannot be read as weather has taken its toll on the inscriptions, but it's still possible to make out the grave of Pheobe Harris, wife of Thomas of Eign near Hereford, who died on 20 February 1824 aged 39 years.

> Tho' long bent down by sore afflictions weight
> Her heart too good to murmur at her fate
> With Christian fortitude she bore her pain
> Till death consign'd her to the dust again.

MATHON

The church of St John the Baptist at Mathon contains a tomb chest in memory of Jane Walweyn, a member of one of the large local landowning families in the past. Situated next to the altar, the tomb chest is adorned by three shields and above it is a very detailed carving of a husband and wife. They are shown facing each other, praying at a reading desk which is placed between them. He is shown in a ruff, doublet and hose and cloak with the carving detailing his garters and stockings. She is portrayed in

Here lyeth y Body of ELIZ: CLIFFE, wife of ALLEN CLIFFE Esq.r Died June 5.th 1754. Aged 78; Who desired never to be remov'd by humane Hands.

The floor tablet to Elizabeth Cliffe at Mathon

a full gown, ruff and unusual bowler-style hat. An infant child is shown kneeling in front of her. Jane Walweyn died in 1617 but the tomb chest is so well preserved that it could have been constructed some 300 years later. An angel is carved at the top underneath a large family crest and there are two small carved skulls; one in each of the bottom corners.

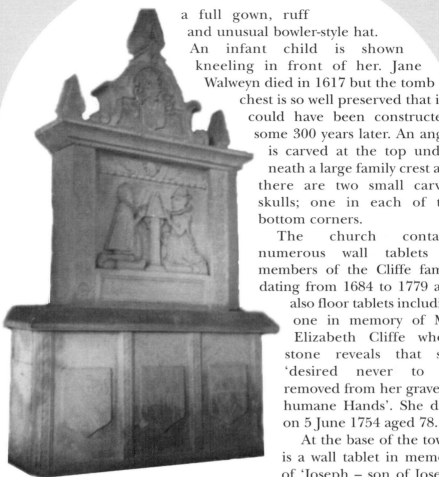

Tomb chest of Jane Walweyn

The church contains numerous wall tablets to members of the Cliffe family dating from 1684 to 1779 and also floor tablets including one in memory of Mrs Elizabeth Cliffe whose stone reveals that she 'desired never to be removed from her grave by humane Hands'. She died on 5 June 1754 aged 78.

At the base of the tower is a wall tablet in memory of 'Joseph – son of Joseph and Elinor Boneale – Yeoman of this Parish, who died August 16th 1739 aged 33'. His inscription reads:

For many days my friends did see
Approaching death attending me
No favour could this body have
Till it was laid within the grave
All you that are spectators here
Prepare for death as it draws near …

MOCCAS

Although there is no clearly marked grave in the churchyard at St Michael's and All Angels in Moccas to mark the passing of Mary Jane Cornewall, her story has been told in Moccas Court and the neighbouring village for generations. Jane, as she was known by family and friends, died on 5 August 1839 aged just 17. Apparently there had been weeks of heavy rain during June and July but 5 August was a hot and sunny day so the teenage Jane decided to walk from her home at Moccas Court and stroll by the Wye. Tragically she slipped by the edge of the swollen river and fell into the moving water. She tried to climb back up the bank but the mud made it impossible to gain a foothold and she fell back and drowned after becoming entangled in the weeds. Jane's ghost, described locally as the Grey Lady, has passed into local folklore and it's believed she can still be seen walking through the grounds of Moccas Court and repeating the path of her tragic riverside stroll.

A stone tablet memorial to Jane Cornewall can be seen inside the church, on the left of the aisle before the sanctuary and past an impressive effigy of a knight. The lengthy description speaks of a young woman of 'an active, intelligent and reflective mind', a Lady with 'an amiable, frank and cheerful disposition.'

MONKLAND

All Saints Church, Monkland, was the parish of Reverend Sir Henry William Baker. The vicar of Monkland from 1852 until his death in 1877, Sir Henry became the first chairman of the compilers of the Ancient and Modern Hymn Book, still used in most churches today. Sir Henry wrote many hymns himself, the most famous of which is *The King of Love My Shepherd Is*, and it is believed that his last words were a verse from this hymn:

> Perverse and foolish oft I strayed
> But yet in love He sought me;
> And on his shoulder gently laid,
> And home rejoicing brought me.

Sir Henry certainly left his mark on Monkland Church, for not only is he buried there but, together with Sir Frederick Ouseley, he designed the organ and gave it to the parish. As you come into the churchyard, follow the path around the top end of the church and his grave, marked

by a simple cross under
the tree near the wicketgate, is straight ahead
of you as the path turns to the left. The lychgate, a brass
in the sanctuary and a window in the chancel are also all
dedicated to the memory of Monkland's former vicar.

MONNINGTON-ON-WYE

The small church of St Mary is situated down a narrow path alongside
the 17th-century Monnington Court. A broken stone slab in the churchyard, to the west of the porch, is one of many sites in Herefordshire
thought to be the last resting place of the famous Welsh national hero
Owain Glyndwr, but this is almost certainly just local folklore. One of
Glyndwr's daughters (Margaret, Janet or Anne depending on which
source you believe) did indeed marry Roger Monnington in the early

15th century, but if you are
searching for the most
elusive grave in
Herefordshire then you are
more likely to find evidence
in Monnington Straddel
where Glyndwr's daughter
Alice married John
Scudamore, the owner of
Kentchurch Court and the
Manor at Monnington
Straddel.

St Mary's does contain
some interesting memorials
however. In the rather overgrown graveyard is the
grave of William Williams
who fought at Waterloo and
previously served in the
44th Regiment under the
Duke of Wellington at the
storming of Badajoz and
other Peninsular War
battles. He died 'suddenly'
aged 86 in June 1874.

Inside the tiny church is
a bust to Francis Perott of

*The memorial to Francis Perott who died whilst
fighting Barbary pirates on behalf of the
Venetian republic*

73

Weobley who died in
1667 whilst serving at sea with the Venetian
Republic against Barbary Pirates. The long inscription
details his life including:

To the unknown dangers of enraged seas
And foreign enemies more dangerous than these
His valour he exposed. Venice may boast
The aid he lent her to defend her coast
Gainst unbelieving Turks ...

MORDIFORD

The unusually named Church of the Holy Rood in Mordiford has played its part in many of the local folk stories that surround the small village. The most famous is the tale of the Mordiford dragon which used to come down to the village to eat livestock and even villagers! The dragon eventually met his end, but until 1811 there was a painting of a 12 foot long green dragon painted on the end of the church. The mural has long since disappeared but inside the church you can still see depictions and paintings of the way it used to look.

The most interesting of the monuments is that of Margaret Brydges whose effigy is situated in the side chapel. She is shown kneeling and saying her prayers, allegedly the exact pose in which she died. The inscription reads:

The monument to Margaret Brydges

Margaret, daughter of
William Vaughan of Courtefield in the county of
Monmouth and the late wife and widow of Will Brydges of
Upleaden in he Parish of Bosbury in the county of Hereford.
Who died at her prayers in the forme as you see her portraiture in
Sorport Court. 14th April 1655 aged 80 years.

Sorport Court may well have been where Sufton Court now stands just outside the village on the road to Dormington. The church also contains numerous wall monuments to members of the Hereford family who have been the estate's owners for many generations.

There is also an interesting wall monument to members of the Bird family which poses more questions than it answers. It is in memory of Harriet Bird aged 38, the wife of the Reverend Charles Bird, their daughter, Jane Eliza, aged 13 and their infant son, Edward Tasker. All died on 24 March 1818 but the circumstances in which they met their deaths aren't mentioned.

Four gravestones for which I searched but could not find were those of William Husbands, his niece Ann Evans, and a widow, Elizabeth Greenly, and her child. They drowned on 27 May 1811 in the great floods of Mordiford in which the Pentaloe Brook swelled after a thunderstorm and carried tons of rock and mud into the village. The four were sheltering in a cottage that was destroyed by the water. A churchwarden said she believed the graves are in the old churchyard (there is a new burial plot further up towards Haugh Woods) but the inscriptions are no longer visible.

MUCH COWARNE

St Mary's Church, Much Cowarne, contains an effigy providing clues to one of the county's most interesting love stories. The effigy of Grimbaldus de Pauncefoot, former Lord of the Manor of Much Cowarne, is located in the south aisle on the right as you enter through the porch. Grimbaldus married Lady Constantina Lingen in 1253 at Much Cowarne, but departed soon afterwards to fight in the crusades. He was taken prisoner by Saladin whilst fighting in the Holy Land and local legend says his captors demanded a 'joint of his wiffe' if he was to be released. Constantina is then said to have proved her love and loyalty to her husband by asking for a surgeon to travel to Much Cowarne from Gloucester Priory in order to amputate her right hand and send it to Saladin. Grimbaldus was then released and returned home to his wife and a life of great prosperity at Much Cowarne.

People travelled from far and wide to pay tribute to the heroic Lady Constantina, whose effigy is pictured as lying next to her husband with her right arm elevated to show her extreme sacrifice. Sadly at some point in the past the two effigies were destroyed and all that remains is that of Grimbald. Both are buried beneath St Mary's.

An artist's impression of the effigies of Grimbaldus de Pauncefoot and Lady Constantina Lingen, now much mutilated

The monument to Edmund Fox, his wife and children

The church contains two more monuments. Next to Grimbald in the south aisle is that of Edmund Fox of Leighton Court who died in 1617. His original effigy showed him lying next to his wife with their ten children kneeling around the base of the tomb chest; three babies were also shown lying in a cradle at the end of the tomb. In the chancel there is a monument to Sybil Reed who is believed to have died during childbirth on 17 July 1624. She's shown wearing a bonnet, with her four children— two sons and two daughters, carved on a panel above her.

The monument to Sybil Reed

MUCH DEWCHURCH

St David's Church, Much Dewchurch, contains the magnificent alabaster and black marble monument to Sir Walter Pye and his wife Joan Rudhall, former residents of The Mynde, the neighbouring country estate. The couple are shown kneeling and facing each other; the detail on their ruffs, collars and hair in particular is remarkable. Sir Walter, who was the Attorney General to King James I, died in 1625. At the bottom of the monument the couple's children are shown kneeling. Although six sons are shown on the left hand side, underneath the statue of their father. seven names are listed: Johannes, Robert, Jacob, Johannes, William, Walter and Roger; perhaps one of the sons died in infancy? This would also explain the repetition of Johannes. Seven daughters are portrayed kneeling inwards underneath the figure of

their mother, but again
there is an extra name inscribed below them:
Margaret, Bridget, Joyce, Anna, Alicia, Marcia,
Francisia and Eliz.

Immediately to the right of this elaborate and detailed tomb is a far plainer altar tomb for John and Walter Pye which is thought to date from between 1560 and 1570. It is still in excellent condition and shows two gentlemen, one wearing a long beard and one a short beard. Further members of the Pye family are remembered with a number of floor slabs in the aisle.

There is another detailed monument in the chancel which shows a woman in mourning sitting below a tree. This is dedicated to Richard Symons and his family who were also residents at the nearby Mynde estate. To the right of the altar, part of a 13th-century stone coffin lid can also be seen in the windowsill.

One of Herefordshire's most intriguing graves was once situated between the villages of Much Birch and Much Dewchurch at Wormelow Tump. Near the entrance to Bryngwyn House was once a burial mound believed to be the grave of Mordred, the nephew of King Arthur or maybe that of Amr, the son of King Arthur.

The inn sign at Wormelow linking The Tump to King Arthur

According to historical legend, Mordred was murdered by his uncle and buried at the Tump and in her book *Arthurian links with Herefordshire*, Mary Andere describes the legend of Amr in great detail, noting that the Arthurian writer Nennius records that Amr, the son of Arthur the soldier, was killed by his father and buried in the tump. Nennius also describes how the tump changed shape and length whenever men came to measure it. Mary Andere suggests the changing measurements can be explained by the changes in the flow of Gamber Head, the nearby spring. Unfortunately the mound was flattened to

widen the road, so the
mystery remains but the name lives on in the
village pub which is opposite the former site of the
tump. Local folk tales also record that it was impossible for a
man or woman to cross the mound twice at the same spot.

MUCH MARCLE

St Bartholomew's Church at Much Marcle is a
large parish church containing some of the
county's finest effigies. As you enter the
church, immediately opposite the porch you
can see one of only two wooden effigies in
Herefordshire; the second is at St Mary's,
Clifford. The effigy is believed to be of Walter
de Helyon and date from 1360 to 1370.
Walter de Helyon's body is buried at
Ashperton with his ancestors but the effigy
was brought to St Bartholomew's when the
chancel at Ashperton Church collapsed.

Walter de Helyon

The lifesized effigy is incredibly detailed
and shows a man with long hair and a beard
wearing a jerkin and tight sleeves. The effigy
was restored and re-coloured by the Museum
of London in 1972. Walter de Helyon was a
local landowner who lived in Hellens (situated opposite Church Lane and open to the
public on three days a week) in the middle of
the 14th century. He left Hellens to his
daughter, Joanna, and son-in-law, Richard
Walwyn, from Stoke Edith. They are both
buried at Much Marcle.

One of the local mysteries involves Hetty
Walwyn, a descendant of Walter de Helyon.
Hetty lived at Hellens but fell in love with a
young man who was deemed 'unsuitable' and
eloped with him against the wishes of her
family. Sadly, the young man died soon afterwards leaving Hetty with nothing but her
jewellery and she was forced to return to
Hellens. Her family were so ashamed of her
that they kept her locked in her room for the

remainder of her life.

Visitors to Hellens can see her room and read the thoughts she scratched on to her window with her diamond ring. The bell on top of Hellens was linked directly to Hetty's room and she used to ring it if she needed attention. Hetty hung herself in middle-age and her ghost is believed to haunt the tower next to her room. The whereabouts of her grave are unknown although it's believed she was buried at St Bartholomew's; outside the church walls.

The tomb of Blanche Mortimer

Inside the church is also the tomb of Blanche Mortimer whose effigy is one of the most beautiful in Herefordshire. The Mortimer tomb is on the side of the chancel next to the vestry door and, like that of Walter de Helyon, is believed to date from between 1360 and 1370. Blanche was a member of the famous Mortimer family from north Herefordshire who were heavily involved in British politics in the 14th and 15th centuries. Blanche was given part of the manor of Much Marcle on her marriage to Sir Peter de Grandison and her

The tomb of Sir John Kyrle and Sybil Scudamore

wealth is illustrated by
the outstanding craftsmanship displayed in her
tomb. She is pictured in a gown and head-dress with
her skirts falling over the edge of the tomb.

By carrying on up through the chancel and turning left at the altar you will find the Kyrle chapel and two magnificent tombs. The Kyrle tomb is situated in the middle of the chapel and is built of black and white marble with effigies of Sir John Kyrle and his wife Sybil Scudamore. Sir John, who was made a baronet in 1627 and died in 1650 at the age of 82, is shown in armour with his feet resting on a hedgehog (the badge of Archenfield and subsequently used in the civic emblem for Ross-on-Wye). Sir John had his tomb chest made in his lifetime and the 1926 version of the church guidebook says the work is believed to have been done by the Italian sculptor Bernini. Sir John served as High Sheriff of the County and eventually sided with the Parliamentarians in the Civil War (after changing sides three times), splitting the village of Much Marcle as the residents of Hellens were Royalists.

In the corner of the chapel is a second tomb, believed to date from between 1390 and 1410. It shows a man in armour with a short sword and a woman in a long gown. There is a lion at the feet of the man and

*This tomb is believed to be that of Lord Hugh Audley
and his wife Lady Isolda*

two dogs at the feet of the woman. Although the two figures cannot be definitely identified they're believed to be Lord Hugh Audley and his wife Lady Isolda, former residents of Hellens. Lord Audley died in 1325 and if indeed the effigy depicts him, the detail is excellent, including a very flamboyant moustache!

MUNSLEY

If you believe local legend then it's surprising that the Church of St Bartholomew in Munsley has not become a shrine to Shakespearean tourists for it's believed to contain part of the sarcophagus of the original Hamlet, Prince of Denmark. The stone has an Anglo-Saxon inscription which was deciphered some time ago by the Reverend C.G. Hunt and Professor L.A. Waddell and is said to read 'HAMLET XHETI AD 362' which would translate 'Hamlet the Jute AD 362'.

Whether you believe the story or not, and modern-day villagers are slightly sceptical about the tale, the fragment of stone sarcophagus is worth a closer inspection. It's easily found inside the church on the right-hand wall as you face the altar although it has been rather crudely surrounded by plaster in more modern times. Perhaps it was brought to England by earlier Viking raiders, perhaps a former Danish Prince spent his last days in Herefordshire or perhaps it was seized upon as a way to attract visitors once Shakespeare's famous play featuring the flawed hero became so popular across Britain? When referring to the fragment of stone the church guide states that 'you don't have to believe [the legend] but it's true that the wooden chest under the bell ropes was cut from a tree trunk and is centuries older than Shakespeare.' Maybe the playwright travelled over from Stratford and came across the inscription when searching for inspiration for his famous prince?

St Bartholomew's is a church with a rich history. The area is recorded as *Munslie* in the Domesday Book and the present church is thought to have been built on the site of a previous timber Saxon church. The church was completed in 1100, whilst the present doorway dates from the 14th century. Next to the chancel steps are some examples of stone coffin lids showing early Christian crosses and a number of circle and trefoil patterns. These were found when the church was restored in 1853, when the porch was also added.

NORTON CANON

The graveyard of St Nicholas Church, Norton Canon,
contains some wonderful mysteries amongst its headstones.
Immediately in front and to the left of the path as you enter the
churchyard through the gate are a number of wooden crosses that
hold small iron effigies of Jesus on the cross. In addition there are
some stone crosses, but all are in memory of members of the Marshall
family.

Follow the path round and on the slope to the left, just to the right
of the tree, are four flat square picture stones, on one is carved a mitre,
a second has a skull, bones and a scythe, a third depicts crossed bones
and the fourth shows an insignia. There are no words or names on any
of the stones, and the parish churchwardens are keen to throw light on
the mystery!

Perhaps the greater mystery is the stone of Sarah Parry which is situated immediately to the left of the church porch. The stone is still quite
clearly inscribed and reads: 'This stone protects from Molestation the
Remains of SARAH PARRY and is consecrated to her memory by a
friend who loved her and respected her virtues. She departed this life in
August 1806 in the 7- [the second figure is indecipherable] year of her
life.' Who was Sarah Parry and why was her unnamed friend so worried
that her remains would be at risk?

The church at Norton Canon

PEMBRIDGE

The church of St Mary The Virgin in Pembridge is best known for its detached bell tower, but it also contains a number of interesting monuments. In the chancel is a large stone tomb chest containing four stone effigies. Two of the figures are believed to be from the early 14th century and show a gentleman in period dress with his feet resting on a lion and his hands clasped in prayer. He is wearing very small pointed shoes and has a well detailed neat beard. His wife is wearing a long pleated gown and shawl with a period headdress and she has a dog, now headless, at her feet. The other two effigies are believed to be late 14th century and show a priest wearing a cassock and simple headwear with his feet resting on a lion and a lady wearing mourning dress consisting of long pleats with a headdress and scarf. All four figures have their heads resting on stone pillows. The parish notes say a local historian called Blount, writing in 1675, attributed the effigies to members of the Gour family, former Lords of the manor of Marston which is in Pembridge parish.

The stone tomb chest in Pembridge church with its four stone effigies

The chancel floor contains numerous stone memorial tablets including one to Dorothy Trafford (d.1621) and Alice Trafford (d.1667). A more recent lead plaque is in memory of Kedgwin Leigh Hill who died on 15 February 1844 aged 'four years and a half'. The lady chapel in the south transept also contains numerous wall tablets to former Pembridge residents but the small brass plaque to the left of the altar is the most interesting. This is in memory of Walter Smith, son and heir of Thomas Smith from Weston Court. He died aged 21 and was interred on 19 February 1661. The plaque remembers him with this poignant poem:

Aged in mind, although in body young
Weake was his body but his mind was stronge
He lived loving and beloved he dyd
Of all lamented, without child or bride
His life was here, his death did prove
Immortal life in perfect lay above
Ripe to inherit an estate on Earth
After his father, due to him by birth
Christ Heavens hyre preventing him of this
Made him coyere with him in glorious bliss
All young men shall be what he now is here
But what he was few young men are, few were
Let every young man live and dye as he
Then shall his life be good, health gracious be.

PENCOMBE

St John's Church Pencombe is the last resting place for an intrepid adventurer from Herefordshire's past. A marble tablet on the right wall of the nave in memory of Richard Jordan tells of a young man

> Who led by a spirit of enterprise and a passionate love of knowledge accompanied Mr Richard Lander in his third and last attempt to explore the interior of Africa and there fell a sacrifice to the baneful influence of the climate dying at Damuggoo on the 21st day of November 1832 in the 20th year of his age to the inexpressible grief of his afflicted parents who in him deplore the loss of a dutiful and affectionate son.

Richard Jordan lived at New House Farm on the western edge of the village of Pencombe and had spent all of his life in Herefordshire before leaving for his great adventure. The church history tells how Richard Lander, who was subsequently awarded the first gold medal of the Royal Geographical Society, led the party up the Niger on two steamboats to open up trade lines. They sailed from Milford Haven on 25 July 1832 but didn't arrive in Africa until October. Only a few weeks later Richard Jordan died of the fever which was rife in the area. Lander himself died two years later after receiving a gun-shot wound.

There are numerous brasses to past rectors of Pencombe in the chancel but the most imaginative memorial can be found at the base of the tower. The marble plaque memorial to Richard Burkeley, a former army captain, 'late of Ludlow' who died 'deeply lamented at the house

of his friend Reverend J
Glasse – Rector on December 15th 1805 aged
48' contains the following elaborate eulogy:

Foremost in Battle, yet to Peace inclined
Retired, domestic, soft, tho' firm by mind,
Kindness of Husbands, Fathers, Matchless friend!
With ceaseless Anguish O'er thy tomb we bend:
Virtue like thine, to Mortals rarely giv'n
On Earth belov'd! Oh may we meet in Heaven!
Best of Mankind, Farewell! thy virtuous Heart
Now beats no more, yet tho' thy mortal part
In cold obstruction lies
Swift to his native skies
Thy Angel Spirit Flies!

Reverend John Glasse, who mourned his friend's death so deeply, is remembered with a wall tablet on the opposite wall. He was Rector of Pencombe from 1767 for 63 years until his death on 13 February 1830 aged 83. He is believed to have been the godfather of Horatio Nelson although documentation doesn't exist to prove the suggestion. John Glasse began his life as an Anglican priest as the curate of Burnham Westgate in Norfolk which adjoined the parish of Burnham Thorpe where Nelson's father, Reverend Edmund Nelson, was vicar. He undoubtedly knew the family and his son, John Glasse Junior, later returned as rector of Burnham Westgate in 1804 and took care of the moral welfare of Nelson and Lady Hamilton's daughter, Horatia, after the death of her mother in 1815.

PETERCHURCH

St Peter's Church gives its name to the village and dominates the Golden Valley community. Enter the churchyard via the north gate (off the main road through the village), and you will find a white gravestone about 20 metres down the path on your left. This marks the grave of Private Robert Jones V.C.—a hero of the battle of Rorke's Drift of January 1879 in the Zulu War. He left the army in 1888 and settled in Peterchurch with his wife Elizabeth and their five children. However, his physical and mental health deteriorated and on 6 September 1898 he was found dead with gunshot wounds to the head. He was aged 41. Many of his friends believe it was an accident although others point to suicide. Local rumour states that he was buried facing west with his gravestone at his feet as he was believed to have committed suicide, but other villagers

suggest this is nothing
but rumour and the gravestone was placed that
way so it could be read more easily. His grave is now
tended by members of the Royal British Legion. The stone
bears these poignant lines:

from thy Fatherless children I will preserve
them alive and let thy widow trust in me

Also buried in the churchyard, although sadly the tombstone has not survived, is local legend John Andrews whose fighting cock called Captain was said to have never been beaten. John Andrews died in 1799 and Captain was buried with him, the grave believed to be to the left of the north gate as you enter the churchyard. The stone is no longer visible, but Roy Palmer quotes the inscription in his book *Herefordshire Folklore*:

Alas, poor Captain, winged by cruel death,
He pecked in ain, o'ermatched, resigned his breath,
Lov'd social mirth, none dare his word distrust,
Sincere in friendship, and was truly just.

The village cockpit was originally situated behind the Boughton Arms.

ROSS-ON-WYE

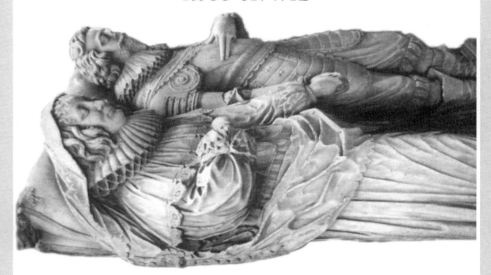

John Rudhall and his wife, St Mary's Church, Ross-on-Wye

St   Mary's   Church

contains numerous memorials to local digni-
taries including alabaster effigies of Judge William
Rudhall, who died in 1520, and his wife. William was the
Attorney-General to Henry VIII and numerous saints are
depicted on the tomb chest. His descendants are also marked with
effigies, statues and memorials including John Rudhall (d.1636) and
his wife whose effigies show amazing detail, and Colonel William
Rudhall (d.1651) who has a very distinctive standing statue portraying
him in Roman armour looking down rather arrogantly on the memorials to his family. Judge William's son, also called William, founded the
almshouses in Church Street in the town before his death in 1609.

There is also a monument to John Kyrle, the Man of Ross, which was
erected in 1776 two years after his death. Kyrle, who was born in 1637,
was a wealthy man who preferred to live modestly and spent his life
giving generously to the town of Ross and its people. He brought a
water supply to the town, repaired the Wilton Bridge, built the public
gardens called The Prospect alongside the church and also repaired the church spire. His tomb, however, is contained within Much Marcle church.

The grave of the actress Noele Gordon

The extensive graveyard alongside St Mary's also contains memorials to some of the more recently remem-bered people of Ross. If you walk from west end of the church (by the tower), along-side The Prospect and then turn right at the end of the Prospect wall you will find the grave of Noele Gordon towards the far end on the left-hand side of the path. She was an actress who appeared in the long-running soap opera *Crossroads* and lived at the nearby Weirend. She died on 14 April 1985 and her grave-stone bears this inscription:

In loving memory of Dear
Nolly who devoted her life to her career. Her
personality and ability established her as a national figure
in British entertainment and she is deeply missed by us all.

If you retrace your steps up to the main path and continue to the right before turning right at the next junction, you will find the grave of another entertainer. Approximately 30 metres down on the left, just beneath a chestnut tree, is the white gravestone of Harry Diamond. Harry, who died in 1907, was a popular entertainer of the time who played the banjo and sang. In the summer he made his living by singing in seaside resorts and then moved back to Ross in the winter where he would scrape a living by singing and teaching. He died without a penny to his name, but a collection was taken to erect his gravestone which shows a banjo with a broken string. The inscription reads simply: 'Erected by a few friends.'

A few metres away from Harry Diamond, in the garden of remem-brance for those who are cremated, lies a tablet in memory of the great playwright Denis Potter. Potter's work, although often controversial, is widely regarded as some of the best writing for television that there's ever been. Born in the nearby Forest of Dean, he spent 30 years living in Ross-on-Wye and is fondly remembered. His most famous works included *Blue Remembered Hills, Pennies from Heaven, The Singing Detective* and *Black Eyes*. His last two works were *Karaoke* and *Cold Lazarus*. Denis, who was born on 17 May 1935, died on 7 June 1994 aged 59. His wife Margaret, who died just a few days before him on 29 May 1994, has her memorial plaque along-side him. Their remembrance stones simply read 'All the way to heaven is heaven.' and 'All of it a kiss'.

*The grave of the entertainer
Harry Diamond*

SAINT MARGARET'S

The small hamlet of St Margaret's has taken its name from the small, medieval parish church and it is worth going inside the church to see the amazing 16th-century rood screen. A Bronze Age burial mound and Neolithic burial chamber have been found in the area surrounding the hamlet, so it's obvious St Margaret's has been a place of habitation for many years.

In the churchyard is the grave of Harriet Powell, an interesting local character. If you follow the path to the right of the church porch and go beyond the yew tree, down to the south-east, you can find her grave although the area surrounding it is rather overgrown. Harriet Powell, who died in 1910 aged 77, was the district nurse and she earned the amazing record of having attended 526 births without the loss of a mother. This is a remarkable feat and one recorded on her gravestone.

Close to the car park is the grave of Robert Cole who died on 5 September 1960 aged 69. He was a famous long distance runner who competed against the legendary Guvussi at Powederall in Scotland. Local people still speak of the way in which he used to keep his training bicycle hanging on his living room wall!

SARNESFIELD

Saint Mary's Church in the hamlet of Sarnesfield is a lovely little Norman church with a churchyard of wild flowers and neighbouring copse, worlds apart from the busy A4112 which runs right in front of the churchyard walls. Although the church is usually kept locked, one of its most interesting treasures is the stone tomb chest of John Abel, Herefordshire builder and architect, which can be seen just to the left of the porch door.

John Abel was a master craftsman responsible for the market halls at

The carving on the top of John Abel's tomb —when the lettering was much clearer in the 1980s

Hereford and Ledbury, and was also given the title of King's Carpenter for his work making gunpowder mills for the Royalists during the Civil War. He lived a long and successful life, dying in 1694 at the age of 97, and designed and commissioned his own tomb. Although restored in 1858, much of the inscription and carving is illegible, but it did feature carvings of John Abel, his two wives, the tools of his trade and an hourglass. The poetic inscription can just be made out:

> This craggy stone covering
> (is for an Architect's bed)
> This lofty building raised high
> (Yet now lays low his head)

A full copy can be read inside the porch, but Abel described his own demise rather lyrically;

> His house of clay could hold no longer
> May Heaven's Joy build him stronger.

SOLLERS HOPE

St Michael's Church, Sollers Hope, was financed by Robert Whittington when it was rebuilt in 1390. Robert's younger brother is far better known though, as Sollers Hope was apparently the starting point for Dick Whittington's trek to the capital city to achieve his ambition of becoming Lord Mayor of London. Although other parishes lay claim to be the birthplace of the historical character now immortalised in pantomime, Sollers Hope would seem to have the best claim as the valley belonged to the Whittington family for more than 200 years. The chancel windows in the north and south walls contain medieval glass inserts depicting the Whittington coat of arms.

When St Michael's was undergoing restoration work in 1887, four coffin lids were found and the most interesting of these can be seen in the chancel behind the choir stalls. The lid is believed to date from the 13th century and shows a knight in chainmail holding a shield bearing the arms of the de Solers family. The knight's head is turned slightly so you can see the eye slits in the helmet and, according to the church guide, his helmet is the 'flat-topped form of the great pot-helm.'

The coffin lid is believed to be the earliest example of an incised military effigy found so far in Britain and the person most likely to be depicted is either Simon de Solers, who is recorded in church records as dying in 1259, or his father. The picture of a rubbing done in 1936 is displayed alongside the lid and clearly shows the chainmail, shield and floral motifs on the coffin lid.

The other three stones unearthed in 1887 are shown at the back of the nave but are not as clearly inscribed. Two of the lids are very large, approximately 8 feet long and made of stone about 5 inches thick. One bears a shield and one a cross and circle pattern. The smaller one is made of thinner stone, measures about 4 feet long and shows a clear motif of a wide rimmed circle containing a cross with a stem at the base of the stone.

STAUNTON-ON-WYE

The church of St Mary the Virgin at Staunton-on-Wye, which overlooks the Hereford to Brecon road, enjoys a well maintained churchyard containing a stone effigy believed to be from the early 14th century. The simple figure of a woman is lying under a five-leafed canopy but, despite much research by parishioners, they have no clue as to her identity.

The stone effigy believed to date from the 14th century in the churchyard

The church itself has
three stone coffin lids on the floor near the
altar. These are rather worn but are believed to date
from the 13th century. The wall of the nave also contains a
tablet to the benefactor of Letton, Bredwardine and Staunton-
on-Wye, George Jarvis, whose grave is described in the entry for
Bredwardine.

STOKE EDITH

The church of St Mary at Stoke Edith was originally dedicated to St Edith
who held the manor in 1066 and served the former manor house and
seat of the Foley family which burnt to the ground in 1927 and was
demolished in 1957. A sense of grandeur is still immediately felt when
you enter the church, provided mainly by the floor to ceiling wall paintings in the sanctuary and the enormous
memorials on either side of the altar.

The larger of the two is a grey
and white marble memorial to
Paul Foley, a former speaker at the
House of Commons. The memorial
contains two lions holding crested
shields and a flaming urn and tells
the impressive life history of Paul
Foley, the second son of Thomas
Foley, who died on 11 November
1699 aged 54. The Latin inscription
states how he studied law, became
an MP for Hereford in 1679 and
held his seat from that date on. He
was made a commissioner for
stating the public accounts in
the reign of James II and then
became Speaker of the
Commons. He married Mary,
described on the tomb as 'the
daughter of John Lane Esq',
and had three sons: Thomas
his heir, John (who died
young) and Paul who became

The memorial to Paul Foley,
speaker of the House of Commons

a lawyer in the Inner
Temple.

The second memorial
is to Edward Foley (16 March 1747 to 22 June
1803) and Eliza Maria Foley (who died on 9 July 1805
aged 46) and is made of white and grey marble with the
family shield at the top. Eliza's mother was Elizabeth Hodgetts,
the daughter of William Foley, so the couple were obviously distant
relatives.

The nave contains a number of wall tablets to other members of the Foley family and to Tom Onslow the son of a former rector who was killed in action in 1917. It's the floor of the nave that gives us the best examples of the social history of Stoke Edith, however, with numerous floor tablets to the Wickins family. The line starts with Mr John Wickins, a 'Citizen of London who lived 75 years and dyed April 9th 1686'. There are also tablets to the Reverend John Wickins, a rector of the parish for 34 years who died in 1719 aged 74, his son-in-law the Reverend Thomas Harrison who died in October 1720 aged 59, the Reverend Nicholas Wickins, another Rector of the parish who died on 2 May 1733, and his only son, the Reverend Thomas Wickins, who was rector for 20 years before his death in 1787 aged 57 years. The Wickins family appeared to have quite a monopoly on the position of rector of Stoke Edith!

Opposite the entrance to the church is an alabaster effigy of a lady, believed to be a member of the Walwyn family, whose new tomb chest is now protected by 18th-century railings. The effigy is portrayed wearing a horned and veiled headdress and has two small dogs at her feet. The effigy, which is quite simple but in good condition, was originally situated on an altar tomb on the south side of the church according to parish records and is believed to date from 1470.

Alabaster effigy believed to represent a member of the Walwyn family

STOKE LACY

The Church of St Peter and St Paul in Stoke Lacy is a delightful mix of old and new and contains some unique memorials. The Morgan family who founded the Morgan car company in Malvern hail from the village and their influence can be seen throughout the church and churchyard.

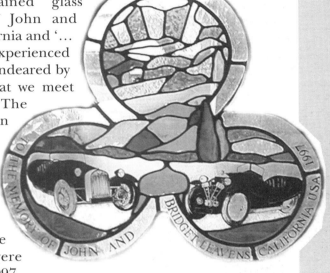

The church porch contains a modern clover-leaf shaped stained glass window in memory of John and Bridget Leavens of California and '… to all those who have experienced the love and friendship endeared by the Morgan car. Pray that we meet merrily in heaven.' The window shows two Morgan sports cars and the Malvern Hills and has a wonderful story behind it. The Leavens visited Stoke Lacy in 1995 due to their interest in the Morgan car and loved the village. Sadly, they were killed in an accident in 1997 and subsequently the parishioners learned that the couple had left £5,000

The memorial window in the porch 'to all those who have experienced … the Morgan car'

to the church in their will. The window was erected in their memory and shows their unusual red three-wheeled Morgan. In February 2005 a new window in the same style was also unveiled in memory of Henry Morgan who died in 2004.

Henry George Morgan, who's son founded the car company, was Rector of Stoke Lacy between 1887 and 1937, and his descendant Henry Morgan followed in his footsteps as rector between 1971 and 1986/7. The family graves can be seen in the churchyard in a plot surrounded by iron railings next to the main path. The church also contains many stained glass windows erected in memory of members of the Morgan family, dated from 1825 to 1956.

A number of other memorials inside the church have stories to tell. Next to the chancel there is a brass to Captain Edward Kempson of the 26th Cameronians and son of the Reverend William Brooke Kempson,

another former rector of
Stoke Lacy. Captain Kempson died on a
steamship on 14 October 1868 after contracting dysentery whilst serving in Abyssinia. He was aged 32 and was buried at sea some 40 miles due west of Ajaccio on Corsica.

To the left of the altar is a memorial to Jane Lilly the 'relict' (widow) of John Lilly which contains a very elaborate inscription which reads rather like a novel: 'distinguished by intelligence and elegance of manners – The sublimer doctrines of divinity were no less her study than polite literature'.

Her husband's memorial is similarly detailed and elaborate and can be seen to the right of the rood screen. John Lilly was an Archdeacon of Hereford and a rector and he's described as 'a man whose truly Christian character and highly beneficial services to the country ... obtained for him the enviable distinction of general and sincere respect.' He died on 30 October 1825 aged 55.

STOKE PRIOR

St Luke's Church in Stoke Prior is full of tiny clues to the past of this typical Herefordshire village. The stained glass window in the south wall shows St Luke, the patron saint of healing, and is in memory of Dr Fairchild Watling, a physician and mayor of nearby Leominster in 1839. Dr Watling was present at the famous ducking of poor Jenny Pipes at Kenwater Bridge in 1809. The ducking stool used can still be seen on display at Leominster Priory.

Tucked away in the porch are the remains of a gravestone to William Watson, a former rector who died in 1688, and his wife, Cecilia, who died in 1705. His stone has engravings of floral motifs which form the shape of a bird, whilst her memorial shows smiling suns and three rabbits.

Notes on the church also speak of a gravestone to Elizabeth Howl which dates from 1331 and also a stone with this unusual and charming inscription:

> Take Pope's advice – Laugh while you may,
> Be candid when you can –
> But truth obliges me to say
> Here lies an honest man

Despite extensive searching I failed to locate either grave in the churchyard, but major work on the grounds is taking place and the weather had destroyed the inscriptions on many of the remaining older stones.

STRETFORD

The tiny church of St Cosmas and Damian at Stretford was closed for regular worship in 1970 but it has been in the care of the Churches Conservation Trust for many years and can be found alongside a busy working farm. The church contains two sets of stone effigies, almost identical in style, size and design. St Cosmas and St Damian's church (previously known as St Peter's) is made up of two naves and two chancels and the older set of effigies can be found in one of the chancels and is believed to date from approximately 1340. The second set in one of the naves has been dated as being approximately ten years younger and is slightly better preserved.

The effigies both show a knight and his wife, each holding their hands in prayer with their heads on pillows. The knights are in full armour and hold shields containing a coat of arms made up of three birds. On the younger set of effigies the birds can be very clearly made out and the arms are believed to be those of the Delabere family. The wives are shown in long gowns and headdresses. It's generally accepted that they commemorate Robert de la Bere who died at some point after 1334, and his wife together with their son, John de la Bere, who died around 1350 and who lies alongside his wife.

The church also contains a shrine to St Cosmas and St Damian, the patron saints of physicians who have been widely recorded down the ages as helping to cure many parishioners, and even some animals, of their

The better preserved pair of effigies at Stretford

ailments. There are also
many floor and wall tablets in memory of
members of the Hull family from the nearby Moss Hill
Farm, and a large stone which simply says 'Mr Holder's Vault
1830'.

STRETTON GRANDISON

St Lawrence's Church in Stretton Grandison is a well maintained country church. The most interesting monument inside the church is in memory of Sir Edward Hopton and his wife Deborah and contains a piece of his civil war armour, his sleeve and gauntlet hanging below the stone tablet. Sir Edward, who died in 1668 aged 65, fought for King Charles in the Civil War.

The memorial to Sir Edward and Lady Deborah Hopton, with a piece of armour dangling below

The memorial to John Taylor

There are many marble wall memorials to members of the Hopton, Poole and Parsons family throughout the church and there is an interesting small plaque to a former villager, John Taylor, on the south wall of the nave. This shows an angel and a surrounding pattern of gold and red and is dated to 1679.

STRETTON SUGWAS

St Mary's Church at Stretton Sugwas contains a fabulous incised memorial stone in memory of Richard Greenway and his wife Maud which is dated 27 March 1473. In other parish records he is listed as Richard Grevelhey. The monument slab is now permanently displayed on the wall next to the font and has a wonderfully clear and preserved black-line portrait of the couple. Almost to full scale, the drawings show a couple in period dress. She's shown in a long folded gown and wimple headdress with her hands folded in prayer. Look closely and you can see a tiny dog hiding in the folds of her dress! Her husband is shown in a trimmed gown, and both of them are reclining on cushions.

The stone was originally placed over the couple's grave at the original Stretton Sugwas Church which was taken down and rebuilt in its present state in 1878. The slab was brought from the old site near the A49 Roman Road and preserved in its entirety.

The incised memorial stone to Richard and Maud Greenway at Stretton Sugwas

TARRINGTON

St Philip and St James in Tarrington is a typical village church serving the houses which were once part of the Stoke Edith estate. The chancel contains a tomb recess with an effigy of a lady dated to approximately 1360. She's wearing a simple dress of the time and an ornamental headdress and has her hands clasped in prayer. The effigy is in good condition but access to it is partially prevented by the pews in front of the recess. There is unfortunately no mention in the parish records as to the identity of the woman.

One of the most interesting tales emerging from Tarrington's past is the shooting of a former vicar, John Praulph. Reverend Praulph was a Royalist who in 1644 had the misfortune to meet a troop of Roundheads near Saint Edith's Well. They asked his allegiance and when he replied that it was to 'God and the King' they shot him through the head. His tombstone can not now be found in the Tarrington churchyard as much of the writing on the older stones has been worn away.

TITLEY

The graveyard at St Peter's Church in Titley was once the resting place of Lieutenant General Lazar Meszaros, the former Supreme Commander and Defence Minister in the first independent Hungarian government of 1848–49. Whilst this government was set up as a result of the Hungarian uprising of 1848 against Austrian rule from Vienna, Habsburg hegemony was re-established in 1849. The Hungarian struggle nevertheless continued, to be resolved in 1867 when a compromise agreement was made establishing the Habsburg Austro-Hungarian Dual Monarchy in which Hungary was internally autonomous. This lasted until defeat in 1918, when Hungary finally emerged as a fully independent nation.

The national hero was on a circuitous route to Switzerland in 1858 when he stopped at the nearby Eywood mansion, home to Lady Langdale whose daughter was the wife of his good friend Count Teleki. (In 1887 Teleki made history himself when he discovered what he named Lake Rudolf in northern Kenya, subsequently renamed Lake Turkana). Meszaros took ill and died and was originally interred in Lady Langdale's plot before being exhumed on 5 March 1991 when his remains were returned to Hungary and re-interred with full military honours in the Cathedral of Baja on 15 March 1991.

The grave, which is situated 10 metres along from the gate to the left of the path, was for many years viewed as a shrine for Hungarian descendants and a new headstone was erected when his remains were exhumed in 1991. Many visitors still come to see where this Hungarian hero died and was originally buried. The Eywood mansion has since been demolished.

TURNASTONE

The church of St Mary Magdalen at Turnastone contains two memorials which give us a brief glimpse of a romantic tale from the 16th century. A large stone tomb slab on the nave wall is in memory of:

Mary the wife of William Traunter Gentleman – who died y 26th of June 1685.

> Beauty enricht with virtue Witt and Grace
> And all perfections Lodge here in this place
> She was too good to live out halfe her time
> Which made Sterne Death arrest her in her prime
> Great is our loss But Greater is her Bliss
> For she doth live and Reigne in Paradise
> Her soul is gone to everlasting glory
> Where Angells doo rejoice to sing her story.'

Mary was just 18 years old when she died shortly after her wedding. There is also a wall tablet to her memory on the opposite wall of the nave:

Mary Traunter of Bunsil, only daughter of Nicholas Philpot and Penelope his wife. Died June 26th 1685 aged 18.

> The good, the Faire, the Witty and the Just
> Lyes crumbled here into her pristine Dust
> How can we then enough her death be moane
> In whom all virtues were comprised alone
> Soe sweet a humour, such a grace did shine
> Throughout her life that she was all Divine.
> Propitious Heaven decred y she should prove
> The wonder of her sex in faith and love
> Then immaturely snatched her from our eyes
> Least to too high a pitch our joy should rise.
> The Belt of Husbands hers she did confess
> His friends and He made up Her Happyness
> And they thought all y actions of their life
> Well blessed in such a daughter and a wife.
> To tell you further Who and What she was
> Does all Poetic numbers far surpass.

A similar use of poetry is on the tombstone of St Mary Magdalen's altar in the church is no longer legible but the inscription was copied by a former vicar and is displayed on the wall:

Here lies the body of
Richard Parry, Gentleman. AD 1626 aged 79.

It is no matter who lies here
Thou shalt lie thou knowest not where
Lend this silent pave thy tonge
Twill sadly sing a dead man's song;
How wild youth wanders on to age,
Thus ends the tedious pilgrimage
What remains of us besides
Time devoured, oblivion hides,
Except this owld man's charity
Who hath bequeathed To churches thre
Above his means; and here attends
Dooms busie day among his friends.

St Mary Magdalen's also contains a large alabaster tomb slab in

*The incised memorial to Thomas
and Agnes ap Harry*

memory of Thomas and Agnes Ap Harry who died in the 16th century. The slab is incised and is similar to the tomb slab to the Monyngtons at Westhide and shows a man in armour with a sword at his side, and a woman in period dress and a wimple-style head-dress. She has a belt around her waist adorned with decoration. Just above the man's head is a small Satyr playing bagpipes and the man also has a dog at his feet.

Thomas Ap Harry died on 3 December 1522 but it is now impossible to make out the date of Agnes's death. She was the daughter of Roger Bodenham of Rotherwas and the arms of the Parry, Waterton and Delahay families are also shown on the tomb slab.

ULLINGSWICK

St Luke's Church in Ullingswick contains a rather macabre memorial painting to John Hill on the wall of the nave dating to 1591. The painting, on a stone tablet, shows him lying on a tomb chest with his wife, Elizabeth, daughter, Jane, elder son, John, and younger son, Francis, shown kneeling either side of him. Two other children are also portrayed as babies in shrouds. The colour is still very clear and the family's coat of arms is shown in bold red and white. Inset into the wall at the top of the tablet is a stone skull complete with teeth shown in a rather grimacing pose. Highly unusual and, whilst really interesting for its history, rather unpleasant to look at! Little is known about the Hill family and notes from the parish history refers to John Hill as merely 'a villager'.

The painted tablet to John Hill

UPTON BISHOP

The churchyard at St John the Baptist is believed to contain the grave of the Reverend Thomas Smyth, vicar of Upton Bishop from 1415 to 1432, who was murdered in the church. The circumstances of his death are unknown but it is listed in parish records as an assassination. Local historians think his remains lie between the porch and the south boundary wall, a few feet down from the vestry, where there is a 15th-century stone that has no inscription but shows a carved cross with a thorny stem covering its entire length.

The unusual hexagonal vestry was built in 1880 as a memorial to Miss Frances Ridley Havergal whose brother, the Reverend Francis Tebbs Havergal, was vicar of Upton Bishop from 1874 until his death in 1890.

She was a hymn writer and evangelist who lived with her brother nearby. She is actually buried at Astley in Worcestershire, where she was also born (on 14 December 1836) having died at Caswell Bay on 3 June 1879 aged 42. A framed example of her writing can be seen under the bell tower at the back of the church. Written on 23 June 1874, it reads: 'I gave my life for thee. What hath thou given for me?'

Perhaps the most interesting memorials at the church can be found on the outside of the Havergal Vestry. When the vestry was added, the old buttress was removed and some ancient stone fragments were inserted into the wall underneath the buttress capstone. The three fragments are believed to be from separate periods, one shows a head and a hand, the second a figure, and the third a patterned stone.

The figure of the head and hand is believed to represent a saint or an apostle and in 2002 was originally identified as being Roman. Following further work on the carving, however, archaeologists now believe that the fragment is part of a tombstone and may show a Saxon priest. The identity of the man engraved in the stone is still a mystery but a partnership between villagers, Herefordshire Council, The Countryside Agency and Heritage Lottery has been set up and is working on further investigations into the origin of the stone. The stone has been removed from the outer wall and is now on display inside the church.

The head figure has been dated as being around the period of Edward I (1272–1307), and the third stone is thought to be part of a gravestone found near the site. The parishioners are working on plans to preserve the stones and in February 2005 they had just received the welcome news that grant money would be available for the preservation project.

The church also contains a stone effigy in a recessed arch in the south aisle but the woman portrayed has not

Ancient stone slab in the churchyard

been identified. The area under the arch was examined in 1860 but no trace of a burial was found.

WELSH NEWTON

The church of St Mary the Virgin at Welsh Newton contains the remains of one of Herefordshire's saints—John Kemble. Kemble died on 22 August 1679 at the age of 80 when he was hanged on Widemarsh Common in Hereford. Born at St Weonards, Kemble was chaplain to the catholic Scudamore family and travelled across the country saying mass with catholics who were refusing to worship at Church of England services. He was staying at Pembridge Castle when he was arrested on the orders of the Bishop of Hereford. Found guilty of continuing to follow and preach the catholic faith, Kemble was executed, but one of his followers managed to cut off his hand and this is now held in St Francis Xavier's Church in Hereford. Kemble was beatified on 15 December 1929 and canonised on 25 October 1970 by Pope Paul VI.

His grave is immediately below the preaching cross in the top right hand corner of the churchyard, easily accessible by following the path to the right of the church porch. Saint John is obviously held very dearly in the hearts of Herefordians still as his grave has contained fresh flowers every time I have visited it.

Next to his last resting place is a gravestone of a Knight Templar, identified when works were undertaken at the church in 1979.

WEOBLEY

The large church of Saint Peter and Saint Paul stands at the north end of the village and contains a number of notable monuments to a diverse collection of former residents. The most noticeable monument is the white marble statue of Colonel John Birch which is on the left of the sanctuary, just before the altar. The rather grand effigy seems totally in-keeping with the life of the former borough's MP. Originally from Bristol, Birch began his life as a packhorse driver and trader but after defending himself well against a group of Roundhead soldiers, he was given a commission by Oliver Cromwell and became a soldier himself. After the restoration he lived at The Homme in Weobley and became MP from 1679 until his death in 1691.

When you read the inscription and bounteous praise for Colonel Birch, it's not surprising that the townspeople reacted strongly to the monument when it was first erected and that it had to be protected by

railings. On the orders
of the then Bishop of Hereford the inscription
was also removed for a time and when it was reinstated
11 years were taken off the Colonel's life; he was born in 1615
not 1626 as the current inscription reads.

In complete contrast to Colonel Birch and situated on the opposite side of the sanctuary is a plaque to Ann Webb, her rural life marked by a beautifully carved shock of corn.

The chancel also contains two tomb chests. On the north side is the effigy and tomb chest of Sir Walter Devereux who was killed in 1402 at Pilleth (Bryn Glas) during the Owain Glyndwr wars. He was the husband of Agnes Crophill, the heiress of Weobley Castle. Sir Walter's head is shown resting on a ceremonial helmet with a very detailed Moor's head crest which can still be clearly seen. He is wearing an SS collar which signalled allegiance to the Lancastrian line of Henry V, Henry VI and Henry VII. Although the arms and feet of the effigy are missing, the detail on his spurs is still very clear and a small lion lies at his feet. The shields on the tomb chest are of the Devereux and Marbury families.

The large memorial to Colonel John Birch by the altar

On the opposite side of the chancel lie the effigies of Sir Walter's wife Agnes and her second husband Sir John Marbury on a large tomb chest. She is shown in period dress with an elaborate headdress and he is portrayed wearing armour with a lion at his feet. Both effigies are well preserved.

Agnes died in 1435 and Sir John in 1437. Parish archivists have discovered copies of their wills which have been copied

out and are displayed
above the tomb chest. Sir John shows himself
to be a generous man who left money to the children
and servants of Sir Walter Devereux as well as his own family.
He left £100 to Anne, daughter of Walter Devereux; and to
'Walter Devereux and Elizabeth, his wife, my daughter' 'all the uten-
sils of my hospice' plus his chambers and goods. According to this part
of the will it appears that Walter and Elizabeth Devereux were step-
brother and sister unless Sir John had children from a previous
marriage, or maybe he felt so strongly towards Elizabeth that she was like
'a daughter' to him? Sir John also left 100 marks to his daughter Marion
and 40 shillings to 'the servants of Walter Devereux senior'.

The will of Lady Agnes is equally interesting as she left 'a rich fur' to
Sibylle Delabere; 'other apparel to the gentlewoman about me' and to
Cecilia Dulton the sum of £10 for 'residue for soul'.

The church also contains a stone coffin lid situated by the pulpit.
According to local historians, this is an early example of a 13th-century
stonemason with a sense of humour. The lid contains the carving of a
cross and a mitre, but the remains enclosed beneath weren't those of a

The tomb of Sir Walter Devereux killed at the Battle of Pilleth in 1402

man of the cloth, but belonged to local landowner Hugo Bissop of Norton Cannon, a benefactor of Wormsley Priory. The inscription is obviously a pun on his surname.

The churchyard also contains the grave of Ella Mary Leather, whose book *The Folklore of Herefordshire* has influenced numerous local historians and authors, and continues to be one of the most highly regarded collection of local fables, ghost stories and folk tales recorded in the area. First published in 1912, it has been reprinted a number of times and is currently available in pamphlet form. She was born in 1876 as Ella Mary Smith and lived in Weobley where she first became interested in folklore. She collected her information by talking to local farmers, gypsies and villagers from across the county. She wrote regular articles for folklore journals and books, but her writing slowed down considerably after the outbreak of the First World War in which her eldest son was killed. Her grave is not easy to find, but if you search for the grave at the front of the church surrounded by iron railings and belonging to a Mr Verdin, Ella is buried alongside.

WESTHIDE

St Bartholomew's Church at Westhide contains a fascinating alabaster slab on the left of the south aisle as you enter the church through the porch. The two large incised figures can be clearly seen and depict Richard Monyngton and his wife. Richard died in 1525 and is portrayed in armour with his feet resting on a dog. She is shown in period dress wearing a headdress and both have their hands clasped together in prayer. At the base of the slab are shown their eight sons and two daughters, with two sons and two daughters portrayed standing behind the others, perhaps signifying that they pre-deceased their parents?

Just to the right, in the south wall, is an effigy of a man lying in an arch recess. He is shown wearing a loose gown holding his heart in his hands with a carved dog at his feet. His head is resting on a pillow and his face and collar-length wavy hair are detailed very clearly. The effigy is believed to date to 1350 and is thought to represent the founder of the original chapel, either a Baskerville or a Monyngton. The monument must have been very boldly coloured when new as it is possible to still see examples of red colouring on the arch and blue on the effigy's clothes and feet.

Sadly, not much can be made out of the two stone effigies in the south-east corner of the south aisle as their heads, shoulders and hands are missing. It is obvious from the man's armour and the woman's

period dress that the effi-
gies are from the mid-16th century and the
quality of the carving shows they must have been local
gentry or landowners to afford such a monument. The
damage to the effigies is thought to have taken place in the early
19th century when new pews were erected in the church.

WHITCHURCH

The graveyard of the beautiful riverside church at Whitchurch
contains the unusual Gwillam Vault, currently being restored by the
Heritage Lottery Fund. The vault, which is easily found on the far left
of the churchyard as you enter through the gate, contains a number of
memorials.

The main memorial is to Elizabeth Stuart who died on 17 January
1743 at the age of 71. She was the widow of Elmes Stuart and, according
to the inscription, the mother of Elizabeth Gwilliam (wife of Thomas),
Anne Stuart and Jemima Spencer. Mrs Stuart was the daughter of John
Greed, the Secretary of Tangiers under Charles II and her tomb says she
'stretched forth her hands to the poor, opened her mouth with wisdom

The Gwillam vault in the churchyard at Whitchurch

and in her tongue was
the law of kindness.' Tangiers was, at one time,
Morocco's main port to the Mediterranean and it
became Spanish, Portuguese, and then, for a short time,
British when it was given, along with Bombay, as part of
Catherine da Braganza's dowry to King Charles II. The British left
Tangiers in 1684 but their time there is not seen as entirely successful
as they deported many Jews and destroyed the Kasbah. The city was
eventually rebuilt by Sultan Moulay Idriss.

WIGMORE

The north Herefordshire village of Wigmore played an enormous part
in the history of the Marches and indeed England, and is best known for
the remains of its castle. Yet the church of St James is well worth a visit
in its own right and contains numerous wall tablets and memorials to the
great families of the area. One which stands out from the rest is the lead
wall tablet and cross in memory of Edith Kevill-Davies who died at
Prince's Gate in London on 18 June 1820 aged just 5. She was the
daughter of Reverend W.T. Kevill-Davies and his wife Ellen of nearby
Croft Castle and her memorial contains the following moving tribute:

> Hark, Hark: My soul angelic songs are swelling
> O'er earth's green fields and oceans waves beat shore
> How sweet the truths, those blessed strains are telling
> Of that new life, where sin shall be no more
>
> Cheer up my soul. Faith's moonbeams softly glisten
> Upon the breast of life's most troubled sea
> and it will cheer thy drooping heart to listen
> To those brave songs, the Angel means for thee
>
> Angel! Sing on, your faithful watches keeping
> Sing us sweet fragments of your songs above
> While we toil on, and soothe ourselves with weeping
> Till life's long night, shall break in endless love.

In the churchyard at the back of the church are two iron grave markings, examples of which are also seen at nearby Burrington and at
Brilley. Here they mark the graves of James Bevan, who died in January
1868 aged 92, and Martha Bevan, who died in September 1868 aged 78.

WOOLHOPE

Saint George's Woolhope contains a number of unusual gravestones. Just off the path, around 20 metres from the lychgate, is an iron gravestone to William Powell, partially hidden by greenery. At the right-hand side of the churchyard, close to the north end of the church, is a simple small boulder. Although it has sunken into the ground and the inscription can only partially be deciphered, it is in memory of Samuel Powell of Hayling Island who died on 27 April in either 1905 or 1906 aged 77.

Woolhope's most famous son is buried in London, but he is remembered by a unique memorial situated a mile out of the village on the road to Fownhope. Tom Spring, the former Heavyweight Boxing Champion of England, was born in a cottage at Rudge End, and a cider press in his memory was erected by a small stream in a field opposite his former home. It is signposted off the road but there is no parking so it can be rather difficult to track down the memorial. Thomas Winter (his original name) was born on 22 February 1795 and died at the Castle Tavern in Holborn on 20 August 1851. He's buried in West Norton Cemetery in London. The monument had become overgrown but recently the area around it has been completely cleared and the detailed inscription is easily read:

The memorial to Tom Spring

111

Erected by his countrymen
of the land of cider in token of their esteem for the
manliness and science which in many severe contests in the
pugilistic ring under the name of Spring raised him to the proud
distinction of the Champion of England 1823-1824.
Thou mighty master of the milling set
more potent far than any have met
In P.C. Ring may Mars who watches o'er
The half stripped votaries of the sawdust floor
Protect thee still and round thy laurels cling
While Gibb, with iron lungs, shouts 'Go It Spring'
Boxiana, Vol IV. 1824

WORMBRIDGE

It's not often that you come across the grave of a pantomime character in Herefordshire, after all Dick Whittington is buried in London rather than at his family home of Sollers Hope. At the back of the church of St Peter at Wormbridge though, there is a charming gravestone in memory of a very familiar name:

> In memory of Cinderrella – wife of William Seaborne who departed this life 30th of June 1857 in the 20 first year of her life. Alas how frail we are ...

WORMSLEY

The tiny church of St Mary The Virgin, Wormsley, is no longer used for regular service but is still consecrated and is a charming and peaceful place wonderfully maintained by the Churches Conservation Trust and local parishioners. As you enter the churchyard, the large limestone tombs to the right are immediately visible. These mark the last resting places of two remarkable brothers: Richard Payne Knight and Thomas Andrew Knight. Born at Wormsley Grange, they were the grandchildren of the Shropshire based ironmonger Richard Knight and the ancestors of the Knight family whose iron gravestones can be seen at Burrington Church (see pp.21-22).

Thomas Andrew Knight was born in 1758 (died May 1838 aged 79) and went on to become one of the world's greatest pioneers in the world of agriculture and horticulture. His interest in gardening as a child blossomed into a lifetime study and his discoveries on disease and grafting in fruit trees revolutionised orchard development. It seems quite proper that a man of Herefordshire should have been so inspirational in the early stages of orcharding, still one of the county's traditional industries, and in 1836 he was awarded the first Knightian Medal of the Royal Horticultural Society—bearing his own portrait. Thomas went on to write many books including the apple growers' bible *Pomona Herefordentis*, and developed many new varieties of fruit. His tomb bears a long inscription describing him as a man who 'Possessed a mind capable of investigating the most secret works of nature ...'

His brother, Richard Payne Knight (d.1824), was just as influential a character, in his case on the natural landscape. His book *Landscape* of 1794 praised the natural wild and rugged scenery of England in preference to the formalised work of Capability Brown. Richard Knight went on to become a classical scholar and collector of art, gems and coins which were bequeathed to the British Museum. He built the Gothic manor of Downton Castle on the family's estate near Burrington, but chose the tranquillity of Wormsley as his final resting place.

Near to the tombs of the brothers is an unusual three-sided monument to their sisters Ursula and Barbara who both died young in the 1770s.

The tiny churchyard is situated right next to a busy working farm and it seems somehow fitting that a family who had such a big influence on farming and horticulture should still be surrounded by the day to day life of agricultural Herefordshire. Indeed on one occasion when I visited, sheep were enjoying the rich grass on offer in the churchyard!

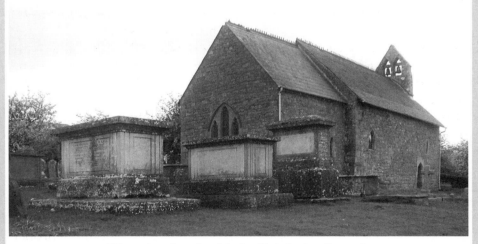

Wormsley church with the Knight family tombs

YARKHILL

If you circle the small church of St John the Baptist at Yarkhill you will find a stone memorial slab set into the outside north wall of the vestry. Although weather has taken its toll and the inscription is difficult to make out, the stone is in memory of Francis Stedman who was the parish priest at Yarkhill for 47 years. Stedman was vicar in 1671 when Yarkhill's bells were cast by John Martin of Worcester. The bells obviously played a major part in his life as his son, Fabian Stedman, went on to publish an influential book on the art of bell ringing called *Tintinnalogia*. The Stedman method of ringing is still used across the country and even on state occasions.

YARPOLE

St Leonard's, Yarpole, is well known because of its wonderfully preserved detached bell tower, but it's worth looking around the graveyard as the stones contain carvings of books, shields, circle patterns and clasped hands and there are some unusual examples of stone-masonry on show.

As you enter the church, turn immediately right and you will see the memorial to Edward Smith on the south wall. Smith, who lived in nearby Bircher, died on 23 April 1709 aged 68 and bequeathed an annual gift of bread to the poor of the village. Known as the Bynors Croft Bread Charity, his memorial and will gave details that the bread should be distributed 'The Sunday before Whitsun Day and the Sunday next after Christmas'. Bynors Croft was the house he left to the parish

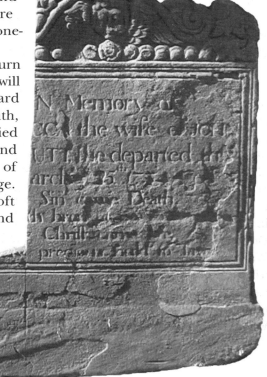

This page and opposite: some of the tombs and tombstones in the churchyard at Yarpole

of Bircher with instructions that all rent and interest gained from it was to be used in the distribution of breads.

The Davies family of nearby Croft Castle are remembered throughout the church. There is a marble monument to Herbert Kevill-Davies who died of wounds received at Ypres on 15 May 1915. The monument was erected by his mother, sister and brother. The Chapel of St Francis in the side aisle is dedicated to Dorothy K. Davies and her son William K. Davies (1911 to 1942) who was killed in action. The east window and a marble tablet near the altar are in memory of W.A.S.H. Kevill Davies.

Bibliography

Godwin, Francis *The Man in the Moone,* Logaston Press (1996)

Herefordshire Federation of Women's Institutes *The Herefordshire Village Book,* Countryside Books (1999)

Howard-Jones, Jill *Secret Hereford*, S B Publications (1993)

Howes, Nic *Herefordshire Curiosities — Outings to the rare and strange,* Arch Publishing (1990)

Jones, Revd. D.E. *The Story of Aconbury*, Adams and Sons

Leonard, John *Churches of Herefordshire and their Treasures*, Logaston Press (2000, reprint 2006)

Plomer, William (ed.) *Kilvert's Diary 1870–1879*, Penguin Books (1977)

Raven, Michael *A Guide to Herefordshire,* Michael Raven (1996)

Shoesmith, Ron and Ruth Richardson *A Definitive History of Dore Abbey,* Logaston Press (2000)

Index